East Riding of Yorkshire

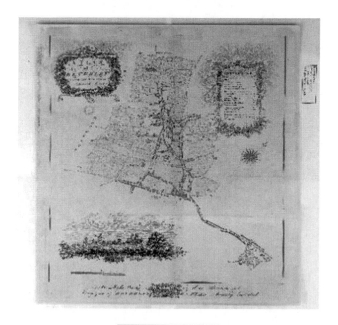

Map of Beverley

THE GALILEE BELL:

From Sanctuary to Asylum and Back
– The Role of the Church

GEOFFREY CARE

BALBOA.PRESS

A DIVISION OF HAY HOUSE

In his earlier works *Migrants and the Courts: A Century of Trial and Error?* and Chapter 12 in the Ashgate Research Companion to Migration Law, Theory and Policy – *'Disowned in their Own Land: The Courts and Protection of the Internally Displaced Person'* Care considers the role of the law and the courts in the protection of those rendered homeless through no choice of their own, the vulnerable refugee and otherwise displaced person.

In this book he outlines the role of the church in Sanctuary throughout the ages and posits the effects of that role in its relationship to asylum in present times.

Balboa Press books may be ordered through booksellers or by contacting:

Balboa Press
A Division of Hay House
1663 Liberty Drive
Bloomington, IN 47403
www.balboapress.co.uk
UK TFN: 0800 0148647 (Toll Free inside the UK)
UK Local: (02) 0369 56325 (+44 20 3695 6325 from outside the UK)

Print information available on the last page.

ISBN: 978-1-9822-8684-2 (sc)
ISBN: 978-1-9822-8685-9 (e)

Balboa Press rev. date: 03/07/2023

CONTENTS

ACKNOWLEDGEMENTS

The local library is a boon to so many; particularly is it a life raft to many of the lonely and those who live in remote places, often relying on a mobile library service. As the British Library puts it, libraries are there for research inspiration and enjoyment. Some local libraries recognise the inspiration and enjoyment but not the needs of many writers and researchers. I am happy to take this opportunity to say that the Lerwick Library in Shetland do recognize all three. I owe to them a debt of gratitude for their cheerful and industrious assistance in my research for this work over 5 years – and free!

I am also indebted to local historians in Beverley, Berna Moody, Peter Lee, Peter Hicks, Pamela Hopkins and Martyn Kirby, who, despite other pressures on them, gave me necessary guidance and knowledge. I am also grateful to Helen Trogajic for the use of a picture of her pastel of the Minstrels and the Bulgarian Cartoonist Jovcho Savov for the graphic rendering of the plight of some refugees in his painting, appropriately called after *Guernica*. Helen Clark Archivist at the Beverley Treasure House and the East Riding County Council have been generous with references and maps. I have relied on work done by others such as Andrew Mellas on Eutropius and Andrew Hershey's erudite work on the trials before Chief Justiciar Bigod.

To Jonathan Bridge, as always, he is an inspiration and not hesitant about warning me of danger areas to avoid.

I am deeply indebted to Ann Lazim for corrections and suggestions, on more than one version of the whole manuscript and Peter King, Keith Best and Berna Moody for their suggestions and corrections.

I am most grateful to the Reverend Lucy Winkett rector of St James's Church, Piccadilly, London for finding time to look at what I have written and agreeing to write a Foreword, she has done so reflecting so accurately and persuasively what I struggle so hard to say. What she and her church St. James achieve, among the vulnerable and the refugees is an example to us all.

To my wife, my gratitude firstly for her patience when she was a 'grass widow' and her invaluable help in pointing out passages which were obscure, inconsistent or just may helpfully be put in another way.

Concluding with the usual author's confession and avoidance - I am to blame for all errors, especially historical ones. I apologise to the experienced historians, especially those of Beverley upon whose diligent researches I have drawn; insofar as the portraits of the *grithmen/women* are concerned, none of us were there with them, and can only hope that, if they could read about themselves in these pages, it would neither give offence, nor draw too hearty a laugh.

FOREWORD

The Reverend Lucy Winkett
Rector, St James's Church Piccadilly

As urgent as the ringing of the medieval Galilee Bell at Beverley, that gives this book its title, is the call issued by Geoffrey Care to the contemporary church, to rediscover its vocation as a place of sanctuary for all fleeing persecution. Modern day *grithmen* (men and women seeking asylum) evoke polarised views in British society and in the church. Care's contention in this context is that it is the exercise of mercy that shapes the church's response in an asylum system now, of course run by the state. He highlights the historic and widespread self-understanding of the churches as places of safety and sanctuary, and comments that in the UK at least, this understanding is not universally expressed. Full of lively anecdotes that really bring to life the complexities of navigating national borders, political expediencies, and relying on sheer human grit and determination, the focus in this book is really on the lives of the people. And for that alone, this is a timely contribution to a public conversation that quickly polarises when framing the debate about asylum in percentages, statistics and the levers of national policy.

Every person fleeing persecution is an individual with a unique combination of circumstance, personality, good fortune or calamitous hardship. Perhaps as Care suggests, the only real solution to the forced migration of people and the iniquities that this provokes, is the harmonisation of all border policies across the globe, however unlikely or improbable this seems. But St Paul has the last word, urging the fledging church in Galatia as strongly as he might urge the church today, to 'reach out to those who are oppressed'.

The evolving idea of sanctuary is a story for our time and in this lively and compelling account, the challenge is clear. Learn the lessons of the centuries: find ways to be merciful, compassionate and welcoming, and before pronouncing on policy, listen hard to the people, whose lives speak volumes about what it is to be a refugee.

Lucy Winkett
London February 2023

INTRODUCTION

In the eighth century, Interawuuda was a small village a few miles north of the Humber River in East Yorkshire; history relates that it was the centre of the Deira people who inhabited the area at the time, some of whom at least, were still Druids. It was to this village that a saintly, former Bishop of York, returned to enjoy his retirement.

The man's name was John. He was one of the few fortunate enough to be educated - well educated - abroad as well as in England. He started his career as a cleric at Whitby under St Hilda. Even The Venerable Bede was his pupil. After several years, he was made Bishop of Hexham and later, to the second most powerful position in the church in England, the Bishop of York.

John's retirement was hardly one of inaction; he gathered clerics and established a monastery. He put up buildings to house them; the buildings almost certainly of wood, of which there was a plentiful local supply.

In the four or five years left to him, John's name spread beyond the confines of East Yorkshire, attracting Pilgrims from afar. After John's death, they came to his shrine in increasing numbers over the centuries, long after Interawuuda became the town of Beverlac and the Borough of Beverley. Today hundreds still visit the shrine of St John at the Minster every year; some are pilgrims, others are tourists.

What happened to those early wooden buildings, we do not know. Did the Norsemen burn them to the ground? Did they fall down? It was unlikely, as some historians suggest, to have been destroyed by Saxons, since their incursions were several hundred years earlier. But the monastery itself survived, and so did the *friðstol* (fig 1 and note 1), referred to in the tales which follow as the ultimate seat of sanctuary, but probably a bishop's seat in the seventh century.

fig 1 friðstol

Aelfric (Alfred), then Archbishop of York, found other buildings, of stone, on the same site around 1040. These were burned down in the great fire of 1188, which destroyed much of Beverley as well. The stone had come from quarries at Newbald and Tadcaster, the same stone the masons used when they began to build the new Minister at Beverley at the beginning of the 12th century: the Minster which stands for all to see today.

Beverley became a wealthy town with rich merchants, expert craftsmen, spinners, weavers, and dyers. The farmers, abbeys, monasteries, and priories, such as Meaux, (or Melsa) kept large flocks of sheep, mainly for their wool. Some of it went into highly prized cloth for home consumption and export. The trade produced a good income for the merchants, and a healthy revenue in duties and taxes for the church and an ever-rapacious Crown.

Flemish dyers and weavers came to the town and settled, contributing their skills to this valuable trade, although unpopular as foreigners and jealousy over their superb skills. The street in which most of them lived was named, appropriately, Fleminmarketgate: Flemingate today.

There was town planning, some of the streets were paved (from money collected by the toll of *pavage*). Most other towns had passageways deep in mud and faeces in winter, deep-rutted and malodorous when dry. As for law and order in the town, there was a night watch and a few constables, who were often - reluctant volunteers. Outside the town there was little or no law or order, travel along poor roads was slow, uncomfortable and risky, especially at night.

John was credited, far and wide, with many miraculous actions and events: he was canonized by the Pope in 1040.

St. John's saintliness made him revered throughout the country and in Europe. His name has served both the Minster and the town well from medieval times. King Æþelstan's (Athelstan) attributed his victory in the battle of Brunanburgh in 937 to St John. It has been claimed that the King gave Beverlac its first major charter, which included the privilege of sanctuary to the Minster, in gratitude for this victory.

Bishop Thurstan raised an army of Yorkshiremen, under the Banner of St John, to join King Stephen's army in his battle with the Scots near Northallerton in 1122, the Battle of the Standards. King Stephen won and gave the credit to St John.

A further grant to the town in 1122 gave Beverley a local government of 12 Keepers or Governors to manage its affairs. The inhabitants of the town had been non-free vassals, whereas now, having been granted the right to own land in the town called *burgages* (note 2), they were freemen. What was also important was that a burgage could be bought and sold at will - an early start to the development of English land law - the freehold.

The name 'burgess' had been long in use, it was mentioned in the Domesday book, associated with trade, but a born and bred burgess seemed to appear when land could be owned, and lived on, within the town (Note 3). The records of such burgesses are contained in the Burgess Rolls – few of which remain today. Chapter 19 takes a closer look at this elusive title, and what can happen to a burgess if he claims sanctuary.

Before having land in town, merchants and traders regularly put their stalls up beyond the town boundaries, but when they had land in town, they could set up their shops and stalls every day (except Sunday) within the protection of the town.

St John's reputation encouraged kings, as well as pilgrims, to visit the town and the Minster. The reverence for St John helped obtain the privileges and at times stayed king's hands from the destruction and devastation of the rest of Yorkshire. William I spared Beverley during the Harrying of the North whilst the rest of Yorkshire was laid waste. Henry VIII also spared the Minster in the Dissolution of the Monasteries in 1540.

The Royal Grants to Beverley included tax and toll exemptions market rights and the privilege of sanctuary. It is this privilege, mainly in Beverley Minster, which was the subject of a claim in the tales which follow.

The men and women who came to the Minster to claim sanctuary were desperate; it was often their last hope of survival. The churches offered sanctuary only for a short time, about one month; but it was enough to save the man or woman in flight from instant, and frequently merciless, retribution – a lynching. If they got as far as the church to knock on its door, the north door in the case of Beverley Minster (fig 2), and be admitted, they were generally safe - for the time being.

Fig 2 the North Door Beverley Minster

Fig 3 Kilinwoldgrave Cross

Theoretically at least protection started over a mile away from the church where the boundaries were marked by four crosses on the main routes into town at the four points of the compass. (fig 3 is the one at Kilinwoldgrave Cross which can still be seen in a roadside field on the way to Bishop Burton). In practical terms, the penalties imposed on a howling mob after blood, intent on stopping him from claiming sanctuary, were unlikely to deter them.

Once the sanctuary-seeker was inside the church, often dragged to safety by the priests on duty, out of the clutches of a mob of men, women, even children out for excitement, they would be safe- usually.

If they had come after 1425 there were two doors to go through - first a porch, the Galilee Porch and then into the north transept. Once the priests were satisfied the man, or woman (there were women too) was seeking sanctuary, a bell would be rung, sometimes by one of the monks, sometimes by the sanctuary-seeker himself. The bell was called the Galilee Bell (note 4) and its peel told the townsfolk that another *grithmen* (as sanctuary-seekers in Beverley were known) had arrived.

The canons or priests, who admitted the sanctuary-seeker would be those always on duty to keep watch for anyone who sought sanctuary and admit them. When the porch was built, there were rooms above the north door, reached through a small door leading to thirty narrow winding stone steps (fig 4). The upper room would give the priests a view up Highgate.

Fig 4 steps to canon's room in the Galilee Porch

The Galilee Bell has long since disappeared, and so have the canons – but the porch is there, and what remains of the priest's room.

Beverley Minster and Durham Cathedral were popular places in the North to claim sanctuary. News of the sympathetic welcome and, better still, the food, had travelled far afield, even to Cornwall and Bristol. In the case of Beverley, the safety of sanctuary extended to the whole of the town – unlike most churches, where sanctuary was confined to the church alone. It was not until the 20th century that whole towns in North America, even states in the USA called themselves places of Sanctuary. Nonetheless, some towns in the

UK, such as Leeds, have followed suit (note 5). But the nature of sanctuary has changed. The last chapter will explain its new form.

The great Minster at York, the capital of the North, was not top of the sanctuary seekers preferred havens, it was too public. King Henry VIII changed all that when he removed the privilege of sanctuary in the Reformation (note 6) from all but eight churches in the whole country. Henry also limited the matters for which sanctuary could be claimed. In the North, York was the only church among those eight. Despite this, parish churches throughout the country continued to accept those seeking sanctuary for the next 84 years; until James I abolished it completely (or so it was thought). The parish church was not supposed to keep sanctuary seekers. The law required that they be handed over to one of the eight designated churches.

In the tales to follow, most claims to sanctuary are taken from the records of either Beverley Minster or Durham Cathedral. Both these churches had been granted the privilege of sanctuary by Royal Charter – and were known as 'Special' (note 7). Sanctuary could be claimed at other churches which were not 'Special', but the privilege had to be proved by the sanctuary seeker – if it was challenged. Most *grithmen* were unlettered, and if they had to verify that the church they had sought such protection from had the privilege, they stood little chance of doing so.

The guarantor of security was the church, but it is naive to think that it could have existed without the state's consent - tacit at least. Thus the guarantee was not always as secure as it claimed to be, but in the case of Beverley the deep reverence held for St. John for his holiness and his miracles, strengthened that guarantee and a breach was rare. Even kings were not keen to offend God, but if seriously challenged, they may have been tempted to ride roughshod over any guarantee. Some did succumb to that temptation. The king's officers – bailiff, steward, or sheriff - would have the job of dragging a *grithman* out of the church, and they carried the can' if anything went wrong. The penalties for a breach of sanctuary could bankrupt them, they could be whipped; if they took the *grithmen* from the *friðstol*, they would be excommunicated.

What is central to the concept of sanctuary, then and now, is that the church supplies the Christian qualities of mercy and compassion when they are absent from the administration of justice. That was what sanctuary was all about in the times the tales are set in. It was in fact complementary to the administration of justice, as it could be today.

But still much of that power lay, not in England but with the Pope in Rome. That power was at the root of Henry's Reformation. Sanctuary could not survive the Reformation, especially with its unpopularity due to abuse. Its original purpose became otiose as the administration of justice improved. Though that improvement had little impact on the conditions of places of detention – the gaols – they remained dark, wet and stinking holes where you could be left to rot before the judges arrived to hold a trial.

The origins, growth, development, and abolition of sanctuary, and the involvement of the church in early days, explains why it existed in the manner it did, and why it no longer survives - at least in the same form. The rebirth of sanctuary and its relationship to asylum is the subject of chapter 21.

The records and chronicles of the historians, ancient and modern, reveal how people lived, loved and died; what they wore, what they ate, their work and their play. That is the flesh which has been added to the bare bones of the church records of those men and women who sought sanctuary, over six hundred years ago.

These are tales about our ancestors who cried for help long ago. Chapter 21 looks at our brothers and sisters who cry for help today.

NOTES

1   The *friðstol*. Whatever its original use was, it became the ultimate point of sanctuary, forcible removal from which was *botelos* which meant no fine could atone.

2   Burgage was a plot in a borough, usually of one *selion*, i.e., 660 x 66 feet. It would front a street in the town and the case of plots, say those in Saturday Market in

Beverley, they stretch back to Lairgate or Lathegate. Examples survived, until recently in Saturday Market such as Briggs and Powell and numbers 40 and 41 (Richard Care Grocer in the Burgess lists for 1905 and 1909 and recorded as working and living there. Now M & Co).

3   See cap 19

4   The "Galilee Bell" and "the Galilee Porch". At Durham Cathedral, the bell was hung in the Galilee tower. There is no Galilee tower today, though there were two smaller towers at the north end, long since demolished. There is still a Galilee Chapel. Galilee was the major region close to Capernaum and Jesus' 'base' from where he recruited four disciples, and others, where he performed miracles and spoke to the crowds around; there is also the Sea of Galilee (Matthew Cap 4; Mark Caps 1 et seq.; Luke cap 1 v 1). And perhaps most convincingly in Acts 10 *'You know the story of what happened in Judea. It began in Galilee...'*.

5   Hannah Green of *UKcityofsactuary.org* writes to describe how this organisation *'coordinates, supports and grows a movement of welcome for refugees and people seeking sanctuary. From community groups in schools and universities, **local** councils to libraries and theatres, they work with individuals, groups and organisations in every area and in every sector to encourage inclusivity, solidarity and compassion for people from a forced displacement background...'http://cityofsanctuary.org/.*

6   The accepted date for the loss of the privilege of sanctuary, at least at Beverley Minster, is 1548. In this year King Edward VI dismantled the Chanceries (3 Edw VI c 7), and everything of value in the churches was confiscated - except, in Beverley Minster, the *friðstol*, which was too big and heavy to carry off in a saddle bag. It is still there five hundred years later. But Henry VIII clearly thought he was abolishing sanctuary in all but eight churches by his Act in 1540 (32 Hen VIII c.12).

7   There were four *Special* churches in England, Westminster Abbey, Winchester, Durham Cathedral and Beverley Minster.

Chapter 1

Sanctuary: where it came from, when it went and where?

Sanctuary can be traced back millennia. It would have existed from when man migrated from single families to groups, and then into nations. Today it can conjure up anything from a Donkey Sanctuary to Cities of Sanctuary, or just a common or garden term for a place of safety. It is, however, both as a term and a concept, very much to do with the vulnerable.

Sanctuary or asylum were important in medieval times to hundreds of people in every country in every year, today the same concept, a haven, is crucial to millions (note 1).

The tales which follow trace a part of the lives of a handful of *grithmen,* a mere twenty men and women, who sought sanctuary. A knowledge of what sanctuary was, and is; where it came from, how it developed and what it is today will help understand what happened to them and why. The tales start with examples of its very early use, through medieval and the middle ages to the twenty-first century.

Each of those twenty *grithmen* were real people, with families, friends, enemies and needs, but all the church records show are names, hometowns, reasons for the claim and weapon used, if there was one (note 2)

The tales try to create a picture of the homes they lived in, what they wore and some of the jobs they had, the games they played, football, golf, bowling, cricket *(cryc)* (see fig 5).

Fig 5

There was horse-racing near Black Mill on Beverley Westwood and the pub and dicing afterwards. There were plays, pageants and poems on the streets. Where they got some of their excitement may be different from today – such as bear baiting in Lathegate (Lairgate) in Beverley, hangings, floggings, some poor lad or lass in the stocks, or a scold in the cucking stool. As for general talk on the street, in the pub and at home, it was the weather, taxes and what the neighbours had been up to.

There were constant wars somewhere, the Crusades, with the French or the Scots. Otherwise most ordinary people stayed at home, and in the town or village where they were born. Travel was for friars, messengers, soldiers and the well-guarded rich, who endured the poor muddy tracks and roads and the dangers that awaited travellers every mile of the way.

There were few enough constables in town, and none outside. Despite the few volunteered constables and the night watch, the town was not safe after dark. The opportunities for the picker (the pickpocket) at the three fairs and weekly markets promised rich rewards for their agile fingers.

Lives were shorter, children died early, if they survived birth. There was little formal medical knowledge, what was known a thousand years before had been lost in this country. The few hospitals and sick bays were run by monasteries, abbeys, or priories.

The conditions of sanctuary at the Minster in Beverley were more hospitable than elsewhere, and this drew seekers after sanctuary from as far away as Bristol and Cornwall. Beverley folk themselves were generally hospitable – up to a point – but, like most Northerners, they were an independent lot, at times even rebellious. Their everyday language, a mixture of Norse and Saxon, rather than Gallic, reflected a dry humour. Grace before each meal in most homes would be in that everyday, homely fashion: *"Wi thank Thee Lord for what wi've getten, but if mooare 'ad been cut, mooare 'a bin etten".*

The origins of sanctuary are debatable. One story is that Nimrod devised sanctuary in memory of his son. Though mentioned in the Bible, historians seem unable to identify any such person and even if he did exist, where this story came from (note 3).

Sanctuary/asylum, the need for safe havens, has arisen in every age in every part of the world, the Occident, the Orient, Africa and Europe. The records in the second millennia BC (BCE) reveal a Hittite King providing refuge for immigrants from persecution in their home country; again, 1400 years later, Ramses II in Egypt, gave refuge to those in flight from another country. Ashurbanipal, an Assyrian King, was reputed to have welcomed and promised safety from returning home (*refoulement* in modern asylum terms) to face persecution.

Later, in the time of the Greek City States, a melting pot of different civilisations, foreigners were considered 'holy', and their protection a moral duty. The gods Zeus and Athena offered sanctuary for crimes such as murder and deb; protection was even given in their temples for a slave against unjust treatment by his or her master. Another temple was dedicated to the *Asylaen* god – is that where the word asylum itself originated?

At the foundation of Rome, recent discoveries have suggested that Romulus made Palatine Hill a place of sanctuary for "fugitives". It was the holiest place at the time Rome was founded and was called "Lupascale": Lupa being a female wolf, which fits nicely with the legend that a wolf suckled Romulus and his brother Remus.

The six Cities of Refuge are the best-known early examples of a well-thought-out sanctuary system. Moses established these on instructions from God for *"Israelites, aliens, and any other people living among you to seek refuge from his avenger before standing trial"* (see note 4).

Sanctuary has always been intended to give time to allow tempers to cool. In Biblical days, when sanctuary ran out, a trial took place; it was not the case in England.

The limitation in the Bible, to six places where sanctuary could be claimed, were echoed three thousand years later, when Henry VIII designated eight churches where sanctuary could be claimed in England.

The terms 'sanctuary' and 'asylum' were always loosely equated, and should operate together, not in opposition to each other, being different sides of the same coin. One may ask 'Was the flight of Jesus and his family to Egypt or that of Mohammed to Masala (Yathri was its former name), asylum or sanctuary? Or was it both? (note 5).

The pressure on refugee-receiving states globally, caused by massive movements of people seeking protection, has led to tightened state borders. This in turn has led to what seems like

Tourain rode his horse up the steps of the Minster in pursuit of a man who had looted a precious jewel which he wanted for himself, as he entered the west door he was struck off his horse and fell breaking his neck.

William spared Beverley the devastation which he laid upon the rest of the East Riding (note 8).

Claims to sanctuary had almost died out by the 16th century. This was partly due to limits put upon its availability by the two Henrys, VII and VIII and Edward VI, and partly due to the church in Rome losing its tight hold over man's soul, mind, and daily life. Its unpopularity with the people alone - who called sanctuary 'Sacred Thuggery' – would probably have put an end to most claims anyway.

In 1540, during Henry VIII's Reformation (note 9), the only church of sanctuary in the North of the eight nominated was York (note 9). But even this did not stop the most desperate claiming sanctuary in parish churches. But they could not stay there and had to be handed over to the nearest of the eight nominated churches.

In 1624 James I passed an Act ' *...no sanctuary or privilege of sanctuary shall be hereafter admitted or allowed in any case,'*. Everyone thought the subject was closed for good – but was it?

A question still hangs in the air - did that Act abolish the privilege of sanctuary in every sense of the word? Or did some vestige of it remain? A right to plead sanctuary?

The Act of 1624 may have been premature insofar as any claim to have achieved a developed justice system. But did the Act have any effect on what sanctuary, fundamentally, stood for? To allow a pause to let mercy and compassion have a say.

Nothing was heard about *grithmen* for three hundred years, and England became a haven, and a home, to many people from abroad. The Huguenots in the 17th century; the French after the Revolution in the 18th; Germans and Russians in the 19th; Jews at the beginning of the 20th, and more from everywhere on the globe after WWII.

The plight of the refugees following WWI was inadequately addressed effectively by the League of Nations. Following WWII the United Nations Organisation created the Refugee Convention in 1951 (note 10) to address the plight of massive numbers of Displaced Persons (DPs) in Europe in 1945. Soon the Convention was needed to cover the millions of those in flight from their countries in every other continent; refugees became a global issue. The Convention was extended, both in time and geographic coverage, by the Protocol in 1967 to cover those needs.

In the 1970's among this expansion of claims to asylum all over the world some men and women did claim sanctuary in a church, firstly in Europe and North America and then, some years later, in the UK.

The nature of the claim had changed, it was not argued that sanctuary now was inviolate, if the state wanted to remove anyone from sanctuary nothing could be done to stop it. It was seen as a means of trying to get the state to think again.

When the pressure from the movement of large numbers of people claiming asylum increased from a trickle, to what some termed a "flood", the UK had to act. The Refugee Convention did not form part of the domestic law, even though the UK had acceded to it. What was more, there was no domestic legislation to give effect to the requirement of that Convention. An Act in 1993 gave a right to appeal from refusal of asylum whilst still in the country. As the number of those seeking asylum increased, so did the number and the severity of restrictions multiply. The tradition of hospitality and compassion began to wear thin.

In 1997 a courageous Appeal (later Supreme) Court judge condemned the latest batch of restrictive provisions in the immigration laws

> '... *as so uncompromisingly draconian [that] Parliament could not have intended a significant number of genuine asylum-seekers to be impaled on the horns of so intolerable a dilemma either to abandon*

their claims or to continue in utter destitution.'
(note 11).

2022 brought restrictive provisions to the point where it is necessary to have another look at what sanctuary in medieval times stood for, and still stands for today.

The final chapter examines this question as it re-emerges today. Do movements like *Churches Together in Britain and Ireland* (CTBI), *The Evangelical Alliance*, the *Churches Commission for Migrants in Europe* (CCME) and Reverend Inderjit Bhogal's movement *Cities of Sanctuary*, offer a way for church and the community to work together not only with each other but with government? Are there policies that could balance the protection of a state's borders on the one hand and the need for a Christian and human rights approach on the other?

*

NOTES.

1   Sir Thomas More, Henry VIII's onetime Chancellor, dealt with the protection inherent in sanctuary in his book Utopia.

2   *Sanctuarium dunelmense et sanctuarium beverlesense* Surtees 1937 Covering the 14th and 15th centuries.

3   See Nimrod before and after the Bible v d Toorn K and P. v d Horst PW The Harvard Theological Review Vol. 83/1, (Jan. 1990), pp. 1-29 CUP.

4   The six Cities of Refuge established by Moses on the instructions of God. . .

5   Asylum in Islam and in Modern Refugee Law Elmadmad K Refugee Law.

6   Derived from Welsh. Edward, I used it against the Scots. It was six feet long, the arrows three foot with a range of three hundred yards and rapidity 10—12 per minute.

7   Sanctuary covered the whole town in the case of sanctuary at Beverley Minster. A *grithman* was free to move within the town boundaries. Still, often they ventured further afield singly or in gangs to rob some lonely wayfarer. See further cap 21 in e.g. the US today.

8   From the Conquest onwards, the North had been rebellious. Under both William I and Henry VIII.

9   At the Reformation, the carving of St Theophilus of Adana was not removed from the Minster. A surprising oversight, since Theophilus is said to be important in establishing intercession with God like with quintessentially Catholic, not Henry's Church of England. 32 Hen VIII c 12 and 1 & 2 Edw VI c 5

10   United Nations Convention Relating to the Status of Refugees 1951 and the Protocol Relating to the Status Refugees 1967.).

11   *R. v. SSSS ex p JCWI* (1997).1 WLR 275

Chapter 2

Eutropius the Slave and Cyron the Athenian

I Eutropius

Eutropius was given, as part of the dowry, to the State Administrator's daughter. When she grew tired of him, she turned him out of her household, and he lived on the streets.

Eutropius had been born a slave in Mesopotamia in the fourth century and here he was, he thought, back where he started.

However he was astute, cunning and ruthless; also lucky After a precarious living in Constantinople, an officer of the court took pity on him and gave him a minor post. By diligence, wit, and a pretence of great piety, he came to the notice of Emperor Theodosius, who gave him delicate missions which he carried out to the Emperor's satisfaction. On the death of Theodosius, Eutropius became one of the grand chamberlains at the Court in Constantinople.

One step he took in his clamber upwards was to have a law passed to abolish the right of the church to afford sanctuary – that took care of his enemies.

Meanwhile, on Eutropius' advice, Chrysostom was appointed to be the Archbishop of Constantinople in 397 AD. Eutropius expected that his efforts to appoint Chrysostom would further his own ambitions, but he was in for a shock.

In the course of his rise to power, Eutropius moved to Rome and became both feared and exceedingly unpopular. Tribigild, a well-respected soldier in the Roman army, and a Tribune, petitioned him for higher pay for his troops and promotion for himself.

Eutropius contemptuously dismissed his petition.

Tribigild, and his men, resented this dismissal particularly the arrogant way he had done so. As a result, Tribigild's men mutinied. Eutropius sent a General to quell the revolt, the General was defeated and killed. In the uproar which followed, Gäinas, the commander of the city guard, declared that the only way to restore peace was to banish Eutropius.

Eutropius was deprived of his position, his property was confiscated, and he was expelled from the palace. He feared for his life; where could he go? He had no friends, only enemies. The only place he could have turned to was sanctuary in a church, but that right he himself had abolished.

He knew that the church had resented and resisted that law. But Archbishop Chrysostom owed him a favour and he might be the only one to save him, despite all his wrongdoings.

So, adopting a humble attitude and dressing himself in 'sackcloth and ashes' he entered the Cathedral, and, weeping in front of the altar he cried for asylum. Chrysostom took him into the sacristy, confronted his pursuers, and refused to surrender him declaring *'None shall violate the sanctuary save over my body'*.

However, the next day was Sunday; the Archbishop was to give one of his famous homilies in the Cathedral.

Sunday came and the church was full; everyone wanted to hear what the Archbishop would have to say about Eutropius' claim to sanctuary. The Archbishop took his place in the pulpit (the "Ambon") and drew aside the sanctuary curtain to reveal a terrified Eutropius.

Chrysostom then delivered his Homily, it was very long, as were most of his Homilies, despite this they were popular.

Of Eutropius he said

> *"thou takest refuge in a Church, do not seek shelter merely in the place but in the spirit of the place. For the church is not wall and roof but faith and life. Do not tell me that the man having been surrendered by the church; if he had not abandoned the church, he would not have been surrendered. Do not say that he fled here for refuge and then was given up: the church did not abandon him, but he abandoned the church."* (Note 1)

So that was the end – or nearly the end – for Eutropius. The civil authorities arrested him. He was taken to Cyprus and then back to Constantinople, where he was tried on charges of serious crimes against the State; he was convicted and condemned to death, taken to Chalcedon where he was beheaded.

II. Cyron

Cyron was an Athenian noble. He lived in the seventh century BC (BCE). In 612 he had been a Victor in the Olympic Games but later attempted a *coup d'etat* which failed. Cyron and his brother escaped but all his supporters were persuaded to leave the Temple and stand trial, on the promise that their lives would be spared. As a wise precaution against perfidy, they tied a rope to the statue of Athena in the Temple and taking the other end, went off to trial. On the way the rope broke. To the people that was a sure indication that the goddess repudiated her support and that gave them all the excuse they needed - all Cyron's supporters were stoned to death. (Moral - do not always trust promises, or bits of rope.)

*

NOTES

1   I am indebted to Paola Malone's translation and Andrew Mellas' paper delivered in Oxford in 2017, for more of the facts. This paper enables the reader to get a deeper understanding of the role of the church in sanctuary in early days.

2   Chrysostom addresses Compassion in this and other Homilies. The word did not then have the same meaning as today. Under Christianity it came to supplement pity because pity had become equated with mercy and had lost some of its emotive content by others. See further (PDF) Tears of Compunction in John Chrysostom's' *On Eutropius'* Andrew Mellas - Academia.edu Vol 1 LXVIII p.9 esp n.59 p168 and p171. *Homiliae in Eutropium* Marone P 1933.

*

trouble again with the Scots up in the Borders. Jim hardly ever stopped talking, even when he was drinking, when he had drunk his purse dry, he complained, loudly *'Aah, me throttle's reet dry'*. There was also Big Harry the old bullock-walloper (drover) from Walkington.

The Inn was full that night and rowdy. Most people there had been drinking or just keeping out of the cold all afternoon. It took a while to get that drunk at the Standard since the ale was weak, but not cheap. But there was a good fire and the dice-box Nellie the innkeeper kept a fair box – she was strict about that, as with most things about her inn.

Jack moved away from the box, *'Ah've lossen t'lot'* he sighed and *dreamed* (shouted) for Nellie. He told her he would tell the ale-taster what piss her ale was, *'drink it the'sen'* he called. Nellie was as big as Big Harry, but worse tempered, and fearsome when angry, she leant over him and shouted in his ear *"Noo ah'll gie tha mi feeat afor ..."*. Jack was too drunk to heed the warning note in her voice and would not shut up. Unwisely he went on at Nellie and accused her of keeping loaded dice. That was it; Nellie told Big Harry to chuck him out. Big Harry picked him up like a bundle of old clothes and made to throw him out, but as he did so, Jack went for his knife but before he could use it Big Harry threw him through the door and turned back. Jack wasn't finished, he came back and jumped on Big Harry's back. That began a free for all. Everyone pitched in. Pierrekyn said later that it was him who *"...strake a chair ower Jack's head"* which felled him to the ground. There was a good deal of blood in the sawdust on the floor. Someone shouted *'is he'ad's broken.'* At that the fight petered out and Jim, who knew a thing or two about bodies got down to see if Jack was dead - he said *"e ar'nt breathing"*. He got Pierrekyn's Minstrel's badge rubbed it on his tunic and held it to Jack's mouth, there was no breath. He was dead alright.

One of the constables by the town gate had come to see what all the noise was about and saw Jack lying on the ground he asked

Nellie what had happened, by then Pierrekin had gone. He told the coroner later that he did not hang around as he was worried that he might be put in gaol, a stinking hole as everyone knew. That was why he went to the Minster.

Matill meanwhile arrived and told the clerk who she was.

The coroner listened to what Matill' had to say, she agreed Pierrekyn hit Jack, but Jack was very drunk and had pulled a knife, it was him who started the fight. The coroner sent Mark to find the Butter Badger and Big Harry. Mark returned to tell the coroner Big Harry had gone to Walkington, so he left a message for him to come; the Butter Badger, he thought, would be back in the morning.

The next day the coroner heard what Big Harry and the Butter Badger had to say; they both confirmed Pierrekin's story.

Jack's brother arrived and asked if they were to hang Pierrekyn could they wait till he had got some money for his brother's death. So *'Is it just the shillings thee's after?', asked the bailiff 'Aye mebbe'* answered Jack's brother *'if he gies the reet num'er'.*

There was no intent to kill Jack, it was a pub brawl, no felony, another accidental death in a pub fight, this time of the victim's own making.

Pierrekyn only had ten shillings. Grudgingly, Jack's brother said he would settle for 12, the balance of 2 shillings to be paid later.

The next day, in front of them all, Pierrekyn knelt by the North door, formally confessed his actions, Kyssed the Book and confirmed his agreement to compensate Jack's brother. The coroner told Pierrekyn that he must carry no sword, knife, club, or any pointed object. He was also forbidden to gamble or leave Beverley and must re-join the Minstrels of the Town. The Keeper promised him a new Tabor and pipe to replace the one lost in his panic to get to the church. Though Pierrekin did possess a Gothic Harp, a rare instrument for a *Mimi* to be able to play, let alone own. That had been a sad loss, an old minstrel who had got it in Spain gave it to him on his death-bed.

So after all Pierrekin could assist in proclaiming the banns on the following day at the Play about Robin Hood. Whether he was a burgess is not known, but if he were one, born and bred no one had the right to take that away from him. Anyway no one was likely to stop him playing at all the functions.

When Pierrekyn was at the Festival on the following Saturday, Matill' told him that someone, claiming to be Jack's kin, was unhappy with the amount of the amercement (compensation) which had been agreed, and wanted more. This man had got a gang together to catch him when he was piping the watch (they dared not take him during daylight).

Pierrekyn took the threat seriously and told Brother James (it was he who agreed to find the extra 2sh for compensation) about the danger. Brother James' father had been a Serjeant-at-Law during the time of Chief Justice Thornton de Wilde (before his conviction for corruption) and had intended that his son should follow him into the law. James had studied at the University in Padua, came back to London joined chambers in Chancery Inn, where he intended to practice.

However, his father died, so there was no longer any pressure to remain in London, a town Mark did not like — it was dirty and violent. He decided to look for an appointment as a priest in the North. He got a post in Beverley through William le Zouche, Archbishop of York under whose administration Beverley lay.

James' was well versed in church law and was familiar with the details of the grants to the Minster over the preceding centuries. He knew sanctuary at Beverley Minster extended to the whole of the town and even out as far as the boundary crosses, so even if anyone tried to harm Pierrekyn outside the church they would be in breach of his sanctuary.

Jack's so-called family were warned of this and that anyone who harmed Pierrekyn would be heavily fined. Pierrekyn thought he would be safe if he were careful. For extra protection he decided to carry a holy relic, which he would buy from a pilgrim or itinerant friar - a holy man's finger bone perhaps?

Whether Pierrekyn rid himself of the tag to his name of *grithmen* we will never know.

*

NOTE

Some records in the 15th century name minstrels as burgesses; this quotation from one record shows ' ... *it is ordeyned þat no Mynstrall shall play at any wedding or Alderman's feast ... oneless he be a burger sworn & keep scote & lote Within the same town.*" see The Beverley Great Guild Book.

Chapter 4

The Carter's Tale

William Kelk was a flesher (butcher) as his father had been. The house in Fishmarket (now Butcher Row) where he lived and worked had been home to his father and his grandfather. The original house was burnt down in the fire of 1188. It had been rebuilt and repaired on that same plot, in stone and later with some brick from the brickfields at Beckside.

Kelk kept his pickling tubs, meat, fat and hay in the back along with his small cart, as a freeman he kept 50 sheep on the Westwood, all enough to bring his tax assessment to £3 a year.

He now put his stall outside the house in Fishmarketgate each day, no longer like his grandfather, outside the north gate. He was also one of the first traders in town who lived with his family upstairs over his workplace.

William Kelk was not a popular man. It was the custom for butchers to sell the offal and bones very cheaply, or even give them away to the poor, but not William; every bit of every beast he slaughtered was used, sold in his shop or used by his wife. Even the bones were boiled for the jelly in her pork pies. If there was anything left he sold it to the farmer for fertilizer.

The mummery put on by the Butchers' gild in the Corpus Christi Pageant held the previous year had been a disaster; the whole town was still laughing. It came last in the competition, the players forgot their lines, most were drunk, as they finished the wheel of the waggon (or pageant as it was called locally) came off. There was a pile of drunken butchers on the ground, struggling to get up on their feet. The gild Alderman was furious and fined every butcher who had anything to do with the play 2sh 6d.each.

What Kelk least liked was being laughed at. His wife never let it rest either, she felt her husband had humiliated her.

Mary, Kelk's wife, had a little better reputation than her husband; she was a shrew, given to fighting in the street - especially with Meg who owned the pie shop down the street. Mary complained of the smells from the fish market, and Meg's pie shop, and Meg complained of the stink from the butchery.

Mary, however, did a good trade in her pies and carlings, which she sold in the Saturday Market, not just in the weekend before Palm Sunday, but all year round. The flitches of bacon and ham she smoked were popular with the rich folk. Come November, she did her cooking and smoking day and night ready for *'Kissymas'*. She boasted she was 'by appointment' for all the lords and ladies in the big houses. She thought of little else but money.

Back to William Kelk and what happened one bright summer's day when he needed more pigs to slaughter and butcher ready for the Saturday Market. He usually got pigs and sheep from the Abbey at Melsa (Meaux). He sent a message to Hugh, the carter, to come to fetch them for him and when he came, he gave him 30sh. Hugh regularly plied between Melsa, some nearby villages, and Beverley. Kelk told him to give the money to Brother Wilfred at Melsa and be sure to bring the pigs back before nightfall as he wanted to slaughter them that same day.

Melsa Abbey was a large farm of several hundred acres and at least five hundred sheep, supplying wool to Beverley, but it also kept pigs for local butchers like Kelk. The Abbey had suffered in the recent famine but had quickly recovered.

Hugh put the money in his purse and set off. He was dozing quietly listening to the comforting click- clack of the cartwheels,

Chapter 5

The Wheelwright's Tale

George Hopper lived in the village of Molescroft near Beverley. He and his two little sisters had survived the great plague, the only ones of the household to come through. His parents, his elder brother, close aunts, and uncles had all been taken by the pestilence. Those people with the funny, but frightening, masks came one day and burnt everything and took the bodies away. They did not burn the house itself, so they had a roof, albeit a leaky one, over their heads.

George was seven at the time and his sisters five and two. The younger one was lame and hobbled around on a stick. Luckily a cousin from the nearby town of Beverley had survived and, though not completely recovered from a dose of the plague, (it had left him with terrible sores), he made sure his orphaned cousins in Molescroft did not starve. A year later however he died. George had to mind his family by himself. It was winter and food and fuel to keep warm was hard to come by. How to get money was difficult for a young lad like him, he would not steal, nor would he beg, he knew if he was caught he could be put in gaol or hanged and then there would be no one to care for his little sisters.

After the plague, land was left uncultivated and livestock roamed untended in the country, there were many cows around Molescroft and Lekonfield, where almost half the people had died in the plague; it was the same everywhere else.

Gathering and tenting stray animals was a way to avoid starving. There were dozens of orphaned children like George fighting for every scrap of food, or clothing, or some cattle or livestock to mind. The strongest survived, the rest starved and died. George found and rounded up three cows and a donkey and tented them hoping no one claimed them, or more likely stole them from him. So George and his sisters fed off the milk from the cows and, when someone offered to buy the donkey, the money from the sale helped buy food and fuel. A year went by, and things were not much better, and one of the cows died – fodder was always short, especially in winter.

George and his sisters managed to survive, George was ten years old and big and strong. One day he was in Lekonfield selling milk. The blacksmith bought some and asked George if he wanted a job to help in the smithy. The smith needed help, there was more work than he could manage since so many of the smiths had died in the plague, and it was hard to find anyone to help him. He said he would pay him 1½d a day to start. That was a fortune to George, and it was a regular job.

He was sharp, quick on the uptake and good with his hands. The smith was glad to have him. George watched and learned about blacksmithing; he took a liking to Tom Killick, the deaf old wheelwright who often came, always smoking his foul-smelling baccy in an old cherry-wood pipe, to shoe his waggon wheels. In those days, the smith had to make the iron strakes to shoe Tom's wooden wheel (Note 1).

Little by little over the months the blacksmith allowed George to help a bit more in the smithy, rather than just operating the bellows, chopping wood, and fetching and carrying. The smith gave him the job of punching the holes in the strakes ready to be attached round the wheel rim.

A local cooper had ordered metal bands to bind the staves for twenty barrels, while they were being finished, Tom Killick arrived with four wheels to be straked. When George was punching the holes in the strakes, he was thinking,' *why not one single band for t' wheels like t' barrels?'*

It looked to the others that he was dozing and told him to wake up; at that George blurted out what he had been thinking, he asked Old Tom, *'why t' bits o' metal not a band o' iron round t'rims'* got a smack across the ear for being cheeky, but Tom did not forget what the lad had said and thought about how it could be done, how much cheaper it would be, and easier.

More months went by, things moved slowly in the country. Tom felt he needed help with the heavy work his trade involved, and an apprentice would suit him well; he was getting old, he had no children; his wife was long dead. Who better than George, a local lad and bright? So next time he was at the smithy, he told the smith what he wanted to do. The smith was not keen to lose George, but he had a son who would soon be able to take over the work George was doing, and he knew George wanted to get on and learn Tom's trade; It would suit the boy well; he agreed to let him go – if George wanted.

Tom said to George *'Yer cum be ma 'prentice lad?'* George agreed but told Tom he had two sisters so could not live in with his master *'Ne matter ther's room'* replied Tom *'cum end a t'month'*.

So, George collected his few belongings - a few pots, knives, a couple of stools, a fur wrap his mother had been given years before and saved from the fire, a few clothes and blankets and the cows, and of course his sisters. They all walked off to Tom Killick's in Lekonfield, the younger sister limping along on her crutch.

That is how George became a wheelwright. He stayed with Tom who got less and less able to manage all the heavy work in making the karres (waggons) and muck carts. Eventually, as Tom wished, George took over the business when Tom died.

George did well, he got a reputation as the best wheelwright, as far away as Driffield and even was getting jobs from Malton and Weighton. Soon he too needed an apprentice, so he took an orphan he felt sorry for, though his choice did not work out well. One day he caught him stealing, another time, he found him trying to put his hand up his elder sister's skirts.

The job of first cutting and planing the *exbeds* (axle beds) (fig.8) was often given to apprentices after two or three years, and George thought he would try his apprentice out on cutting and rough planing a new ex-bed for a muck cart for Malton.

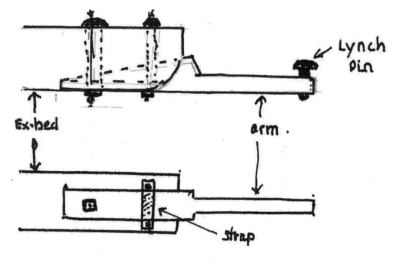

Fig 8 Ex-bed

George had to go to Beverley to repair a karre, so he left the boy to try his hand. He returned a bit earlier than he expected and found the apprentice using George's own tools. Angrily he shouted at him just as the boy was bringing down the axe, it hit the wood, glanced off, and the blade cut deeply into his groin. The blood spurted up to the beams of the low roof, the boy screamed and fell to the floor; George just stood there for a minute, shocked, he then knelt down, so he said later, ripped off the boy's shirt to try to stop the flow of blood; pressing on the wound as hard as he could but the flow would not stop; the boy died.

Every wheelwright made his own tools, this was important. The bias of the ash shaft was different for a left-handed man than it was for a right-handed one. Also, the edge of the adze or the axe had to be ground on the unconforming (the opposite) side if you were left-handed, and George was left-handed. A right-handed man cannot safely use the tools made for a left-handed man. Not only will the edges be blunted, but there is the danger that the axe may slip, and when it does, it can slide down into the user's thigh and cause a nasty cut. Just as it had happened that very moment.

Maybe all the lad would have got would have been a reprimand and a thrashing, but this had been the last straw. George finding him using his (George's) tools he lost his temper, shouted and raised his hand to him – he did not hit the boy.

George knew he was not guilty of the boy's death but if he reported the death the constable would arrest him and take him to gaol where, at best, he may languish, awaiting trial, for years. As likely as not he would die there or come out disabled, like the woman in Weel a few months ago whose foot rotted off in gaol. The gaols had a disgusting reputation, and the gaolers were worse than the people they were supposed to guard. What was worse, he would be unable to care for his sisters.

So, what to do?

He wrapped the boy's body in an old blanket and, waiting for dusk, took the body in his cart and buried the boy in the woods a mile or so away. If he were asked where his apprentice was, he would tell them the boy was so useless that he had sacked him and had just run off.

The boy was never heard of again - and no one was much bothered either. But George's conscience bothered him.

He lived with it for seven years; in the meantime, his sisters married and moved off to nearby villages.

The time came when he could stand the remorse no longer. So, one morning he closed his workshop and the house, and went to Beverley Minster. He banged on the north door and when the monk opened it he told him that he wanted protection.

He confessed the crime, paid 4d to the clerk and 2sh 4d to the bailiff, Kyssed the Book, and made his oath of fealty to the abbot.

George knew that he must leave the church after 40 days and when he did, he may have to await his trial for years in gaol. If he were convicted at all, even of hiding the boy's body, he could be put is a gaol. The alternative was to leave the country, unless the church would take him in.

After the coroner had taken George's oath in the presence of three canons of the church, George knelt and asked forgiveness from God, promising to undergo whatever penance God required of him. At that moment a shaft of light pierced a window and fell on the altar by which he was kneeling.

The Prior conferred with the canons and the coroner, it was agreed God had spoken. He told George *'It is clear God has forgiven you and the penance decreed is that you give the rest of your life to the church'*.

He would seek a pardon for him anyway, but as it happened, it never came.

George stayed at the Minster for the rest of his life. He repaired their waggons, the tumbril, water, and muck carts and ensured the church 'pageant' (originally pageant was the waggon itself) always ready for the plays. He died just after the turn of the century, an old man, well-contented with his life of service to the church for a quarter of a century.

*

NOTE

1   In medieval times, wheelwrights fixed a series of plates to the outer rim of the wooden wheels for farm, or wagons (Karres), not a single band of metal, as George suggested, on the outer rim of the wheel. See the accounts in The Wheelwright's Shop by George Sturt.

Chapter 6

Sir John Holland, Duke of Exeter

There are two versions of the same event. There usually are, and what follows is an example.

6 a. Richard II had a half-brother, John who was part of the King's Scottish expedition in 1385. Also serving in the army was Ralph, the son of the Earl of Stafford. When the forces got as far as Berwick, they set up camp for the night.

One of Ralph Stafford's archers had left camp to go on a binge in Berwick. He came back to camp drunk. On the way to his bivouac in Ralph's lines, one of John Holland's squires saw the archer weaving his way through the lines of the camp, he went over to him grabbed his arm and demanded to know where he had been. The archer stumbled and vomited all over the squire, who knocked him to the ground and, turning on his heel began to walk away. The archer picked himself up and in his drunken anger, pulled his dagger from his belt he threw it at the retreating back of the squire, unfortunately it hit him point first and killed him.

Another soldier saw what had happened, recognised the squire, and the archer and ran to Ralph Stafford to report what he had seen. Ralph instructed him to remove the squire's body to the young man's tent and marched off to see John Holland to tell him what happened and apologise for one of his men having killed Holland's squire. Before Ralph could explain, one of Holland's men came up and told him '*an archer from his* (pointing at Stafford) *detachment, has killed your squire'*. John Holland, well known for his sudden and intemperate outbursts of temper (which had got him in trouble several times before) did not wait to hear what Ralph Stafford had to say, but drew his dagger and thrust it into Stafford's chest, killing him instantly.

When his temper had cooled down, which it very quickly did after he realized what he had done. He knew that Ralph's father, the Earl of Stafford, would stop at nothing until he had persuaded the King to have him tried for murder – the outcome of which, despite his relationship to the King, was a foregone conclusion. He knew there was one course open to him, and he had to be fast. He called another of his squires and commanded him to saddle his horse, prepare two spare horses, and be ready to ride with him that night.

He set off within the hour and headed south. With barely a pause, except to change horses, one of which, foaming at the mouth, dropped dead under him, so fast had he ridden. He reached Beverley in the late afternoon, clattered in through the Bar, past St Mary's across the Market Place and the Archbishop's Ding, collecting a ragged following of the curious, down Fishmarket to Highgate. By the time he reached the North door of the Minster which was already open as the canons had seen and heard him coming, Holland dismounted, gave the horse and his sword and his dagger to the squire, entered the Minster and claimed sanctuary.

The Galilee Bell was rung, as was the custom, to notify the town of a claim to sanctuary; the crowd which had followed him slowly dispersed, there being no further fun to be had. He was lodged in the dormitory for gentlefolk kept by the Abbot for the Minster's more noble 'guests' to await the coroner.

In due course, when the coroner came, with the bailiff and the clerk, and, in the presence of witnesses, took John Holland's confession to the murder of Ralph Stafford at Berwick by striking him with his dagger. Holland also stated his position and title all of which, unusually, the clerk enrolled. With his hand on the Bible Holland took the oath of fealty to the Abbot.

By invoking the privilege of sanctuary Holland knew he would lose his lands and his right to the Earldom. It was more than likely that he would be required to leave the country, since he dared not risk a trial. Unless pardoned by the King exile would be for the rest of his life. He had 30 days in which efforts to secure a pardon from the King must bear fruit.

It was rare for Beverley Minster to accede to handing over a sanctuary man against his will and rarer still for the privilege of sanctuary at Beverley to be breached forcibly, so John Holland felt safe. But he was not naïve, he knew that if the King was persuaded to turn a blind eye to Stafford's men forcibly removing him, or starving him out, neither the Abbot nor the Archbishop in York could save him.

In those days even urgent news travelled at the pace of a horse, but when the Earl of Stafford had received the news, he hastened to the King to seek Holland's execution. Others had heard too - notably the King's Uncle Clarence. He too made his way to the King, but he went to intercede with the King for a pardon for Holland. When Holland was told of Clarence's intercession he went into the church and fell to his knees at the altar and begged forgiveness of the Lord and prayed that the King may pardon him.

Richard's and John's mother, the famed Joan Maid of Kent, fervently begged the King to forgive and pardon John.

The King refused all overtures for a pardon and confirmed the forfeiture of Holland's lands and his Dukedom. Joan died shortly afterwards; it was said of grief at the quarrel between her sons.

Despite Holland's election to abjure the realm at the end of 40 days, under pressure by the King he was taken out of sanctuary to stand trial; he was convicted and condemned to death.

There must have been negotiations behind the scenes, because Holland was not executed and became reconciled with the Earl of

Stafford, whose family no longer sought Holland's death. The King pardoned him and restored to him his titles and all his lands.

That may have been how John Holland's claim to sanctuary and his reconciliation with Stafford and King Richard ended, but it was not the end of the rest of Sir John Holland's story.

Henry Bolingbroke (a Lancastrian and a Tudor) became King after the deposition and imprisonment of Richard II (the last of the Plantagenets). Holland then entered a conspiracy to assassinate Henry and his sons and restore Richard to the throne. This time it was not his hot temper which got him into his final trouble but his mistake in backing the wrong side. The plot failed and Holland fled, but this time he was caught and no issue of sanctuary or a pardon arose – he was executed, buried in Pleshey, all his lands and titles were forfeited.

Holland's second son, who was also called John, gave his support to King Henry, unlike his father he backed the right side and as a result the King restored all his father's lands and titles to him.

6 b. This is the other version of the same event; the reader may judge which of the two accounts is the more credible.

There was, in the Queen's train a certain Sir Melas, a young Bohemian, with fair hair and blue eyes, "quite of the German type". He had to seek lodging, which, in very bad English, he strove to do. One of Sir John Holland's squires mocked Sir Melas for his accent and made him the butt of rude ridicule. An archer of Sir Ralph Stafford's, passing by took the German's part, and in the quarrel which developed he killed the squire. As soon as Sir John heard that his squire had been killed, he took a solemn oath that he would neither eat nor drink till he had killed Sir Melas. Why him, who was the innocent party in this affray, the records do not relate.

Holland rode about furiously on the Westwood outside the town, where he met Sir Ralph Stafford, and mistaking him for the German, he struck at him with his sword and rode on without staying to see what he had done. The blow, however, was fatal, and the dead body of Sir Ralph, a gallant young knight, was carried through the

North Bar at Beverley to his distraught father. Meantime Sir John Holland, heard of the identity of the person he had struck, and that the man had died from that blow, took refuge in St John's Sanctuary in Beverley Minster, where poor Sir Melas and the archer were already sheltered; so he had an enemy for company.

The whole Royal Court was in commotion; the King swore that Sir John Holland should die and would have ordered his immediate execution, except that Holland had reached the chair of peace (the *friðstol*) in Beverley Minster whither even a king would hesitate long before removing him. In vain, Joan knelt before her son, the King, imploring pardon for her elder son John. Joan was the widow of the late Sir John Holland who then married the Black Prince. Her sorrow was so bitter that soon afterwards she died.

When the old Lord Stafford recovered from his first burst of grief he went to the King and told him that, till he returned from fighting the Scots, he would not think of his own afflictions. *'I like not that the Scots should rejoice in the misery of the Earl of Stafford.'* When the expedition was over, he went to the Holy Land, on account of his son's death, and died there. Meantime Sir John Holland remained in Beverley until the King pardoned him; but not before Joan had died.

The King made him Duke of Exeter and he married one of the daughters of John of Gaunt. One is left wondering what Holland had done for the king to bring that about – or was it just that the King had other more important troubles on his hands in which Holland may be useful as a live ally rather than another dead nobleman.

*

Chapter 7

The Ploughman's Tale

Piers was born in Anglesey, Wales. His father had been a pikeman in the English King's army and had lost his left arm. When the rest of the army returned to England, Pier's father and his family went with them, returning to Lund in the East Riding of Yorkshire where he had been born.

His father's wounds made it difficult for him to find work and he was too proud to beg. The only job he could find was as a gong farmer (to us an unrevealing name for a cesspit cleaner). They had a very small piece of land by the woods on which they kept a few chickens and a pig which could winter in part of the woods. The wife mended and washed clothes.

Their home was a hut of rough walls of wattle and daub, the roof of poorly thatched straw, which let in more rain than it kept out! The fire, a hearth on the floor had no chimney, but the gaps in the roof were chimney enough and fuel was usually available from the nearby woods. Their possessions were few; enough straw to sleep on, three threadbare blankets, a pot or two, knives, a spade, a fork, and a useful billhook which Piers' father had brought back from Wales - and the clothes they stood up in. They may have been poor but they had good health with enough to eat, except in a bad winter.

Piers was big for his age, and strong even at 9. He got a job to tent (mind) a local farmer's cattle. When he was 11, he took a labouring job at the Priory at Wartre (Warter). He worked hard; he got a bit of extra food or money running errands on Fair days, he was a likeable lad. After a couple of years, having watched the ploughman carefully, Piers persuaded the ploughman to let him try his hand at ploughing on his own. The ploughman, who was to retire soon, thought he would see how he would do in some wet ground which had to be ploughed up for spring greens. Piers gave it a go and he made as straight a furrow as would it would take most ploughmen, older than him a couple of years to do as well.

The months went by and Piers was able to get more practice at the plough. Come Martinmas in the following year the ploughman did retire. He told the monks that if Piers wanted, he was good enough to take over. Piers was hired; he became a *stattie,* or statute hired ploughman, at 2½d a day for the next year (he could have taken a shorter term if he wished but it was not popular at the time with the employers). He also had a place to stay, with other labourers, in one of the byres at the Priory along with other farm workers. It was not that much better than where the cows had been but there was a brazier, and the roof kept the rain out.

All went well for Piers until, without warning, just after his 15th birthday the plague struck the farm. They were luckier than most farms around and of the six farm hands and the twelve monks and the Prior only four succumbed, though two friars took themselves off to Finkle Priory (a monk's retirement home near Durham) and never came back. The plague took Piers' father, mother, and all bar one sister, who came to live at the farm and was given a job as dairymaid. She brought with her the few belongings which had escaped destruction after the plague - including the billhook from Wales (the Wallych bill).

After the plague had passed wages increased generally, but the Statute of Labourers banned workers from moving to get higher wages. Many did so anyway. Piers continued working at Wartre – out of loyalty - even though he thought that he could get 5d a day if he moved elsewhere. But he could be prosecuted and brought back if he did, and he would, as likely as not, be worse off than before. If the hours of any contract were not fixed it was too late afterwards when you found you had to work from four in the morning till seven at night.

He stayed on therefore until another Martinmas came along. At the Mel (Harvest) Supper, which was celebrated after the harvest was in, threshing finished and corn bagged, he was approached by Sir Ralph Mydleton's bailee. Mydleton had a large farm on the Wolds with over 800 sheep, a good deal of hill and arable land. Mydleton did well out of selling the wool, even though the markets at Beverley were not as good as they used to be. His Bailee was desperate for a good ploughman and offered 4½d a day.

On 23ʳᵈ November Piers went off to the pub in Ryedale, where all the local hiring took place, to see Mydleton's Bailee; he told him he would take the job and as usual took *God's Penny* to seal the deal.

What he did not know was that the Proctor of Wartre Priory was in Ryedale too and overheard the bargain being reached between Mydleton's Bailee and Piers. He called the constable to arrest Piers, which he did, the Proctor should have reported Mydleton and his Bailee as well, but he did not. It was common for only the labourer to be prosecuted.

The constable manacled Piers and tied him to the back of his donkey, intending to lead him off to Beverley and put him in goal there to await trial.

Piers knew that by the time he came to trial he may be too sick or disabled ever to work again; the conditions in prison were bad, they were wet, dirty, stinking from lack of anything but a bucket to relieve oneself in, and that shared with anyone else in the cell. The food was rotten and scarce unless you had money or someone to bring it. What awaited him was, at best a life as a vagrant, a beggar, and a disabled one too for whom no one had any time. Unlicensed ones were often flogged, and what would become of his sister?

He could easily free himself from the constable's donkey, but where would he go? He would be declared an outlaw.

The journey to Beverley was slow. They had to stop the night at an Inn on the way around Burton Fleming. If he was to escape this may be his only chance he thought.

Having got to the Inn it was so full that they had to sleep with the donkey in the stables. The constable chained Piers to a wall ring and went off to get food for them and hay and water for the donkey. Piers thought, he was likely to be at least half an hour. But he was longer and when he did get back with some food, he had obviously stopped too long a time in the taproom; he was very drunk and told Piers to feed himself and the pony (forgetting Piers was chained to the wall) and promptly fell asleep.

It is now or never, thought Piers. He fumbled in the dark for the keys to the padlock on the constable's belt. He got them and had just unlocked himself when the constable woke up and reached for his nightstick. A blow from that would at least knock Piers senseless, so he grabbed the stick from the constable and hit him; he was not sure where the blow fell but the constable grunted and fell back heavily to the ground.

Piers thought that he had killed him, so he took the donkey and rode off. He had nowhere to go. He had heard about sanctuary so perhaps the only chance he had was to seek sanctuary. The nearest place he knew of was Beverley Minster. So he continued the journey to Beverley to take whatever came after that. He was not sure where it would lead, but it would give him time to think – and would avoid that nauseous gaol, at least for now.

The gates into Beverley were still shut when he arrived, so he had to wait. By then he was wet, cold and frightened. When the gate was open, he hurried past St Mary's, through an already crowded Market up Fishermarketgate and finally down Highgate; wet, exhausted, and frightened he arrived at the North door of the Minster.

He did not need to knock; the door was quickly opened by Mark one of the canons who had been cleaning the entrance. Piers stuttered out some of his story from which Mark discerned that this bedraggled young man with the donkey had killed someone and wanted shelter from arrest. He was the third person claiming the privilege of sanctuary in two days, as usual the Galilee Bell was rung to announce that someone else had claimed sanctuary.

Mark tied the donkey to a railing and took Piers to the refectory for some hot broth and bread and fetched the black robe with the yellow cross on the shoulder which *Grithmen* must wear. Mark took his wet clothes away to dry.

The coroner was sent for but did not come for three days. Meanwhile Piers was given some work to do around the church. The donkey had been put in the stables. When the coroner came with the bailiff and the clerk, the Abbot made sure they were well fed and watered with the Minster's (next) best wine.

When the coroner was finished, he called for two witnesses and heard Piers' story.

Piers explained what had happened and confessed to causing the death of the constable. His oath was taken on his knees by the altar – it was too cold and wet to open the doors, he *Kyssed* the Book. The coroner carefully explained he could stay for 40 days but then must either stand trial or leave the country, unless a pardon could be obtained, The clerk recorded Piers' name, occupation, the crime, and the weapon used.

The Minster was well known for it's hospitality to those under its protection and as he had 40 days to think about it, he decided to make the best of it – and meanwhile pray.

His sister had spoken with the Proctor at Wartre, after her brother had disappeared. He had heard what had happened after Piers' arrest, and that the constable was not dead, the blow had been enough to leave him senseless for two days. When he came round, he did not remember what had happened, he did not even remember Piers. Piers' sister and the Proctor set out to search for him, someone suggested *'try the Minster or St Mary's in Beverley.* They enquired at both and found him digging in the church gardens at the Minster.

She told Piers that the constable was alive; this cheered him up, but he still thought he would be tried for something and preferred to take his chances with exile.

The coroner was informed of the constable's survival but, as Piers feared that if he stayed after forty days, he may still have to stand trial so he had better leave the country. He had no idea what that would entail – the hardships, the risks, and almost certain death from something or other far from home.

He was fortunate that the coroner directed that he leave through the port at Hull which was only a few miles away, and he would make sure he was accompanied by a constable. The road to Hull was usually safe in daytime.

When the forty days was up, and no further news had been heard from Wartre, or about the constable Piers was given a wooden cross, with the white robe which he must wear. Out of kindness he was given shoes, bread, and cheese for the journey and a little money for the boat. Accompanied by a constable and a friar, and a crowd of curious sightseers, he set off early one morning. Snow had fallen in the night, but the sun was shining, and all looked clean and bright, unlike Piers who may have been clean but he was not feeling bright. He had heard a little more of what awaited him, he would never see his home again, he would never see his sister again. He would not know what people were saying in some foreign land, and if they hated foreigners as much as they did here at home, he was likely to starve to death if he was not murdered first.

As they reached Woodmansee he was reminded of what might have been his fate, there was a grotesque half skeleton of a corpse hanging in chains in a gibbet by the crossroads. Just then there was a commotion at the back of the crowd, a monk was pushing his way through. He reached Piers and grabbing him, he gasped out his story.

The Prior from Wartre had now seen the injured constable, who had recovered his memory and his health, and was able to recall most of the events of that day. The constable was a fair man, he knew he had been in the wrong to get drunk, and the offence was quite minor, he knew also that neither Lord Mydelton nor his bailee would be prosecuted. He did not want the lad to be hanged, or sent abroad, so he agreed that if he received compensation for his injuries he would be satisfied. The Prior had sent the monk to fetch Piers back if the coroner agreed.

The Prior was also unhappy about the way the Statute of Labourers was being enforced, with only the labourer being punished. So he went to see Mydleton, he told him straight, that if he did not release Piers from the contract to work for him and make sure he was not presecuted, he would insist that Mydleton be prosecuted for trying to get Piers to work for him by offering him higher wages than he was already getting at Wartre. Mydleton agreed – he had little choice.

Piers now only had to pay the constable (and payment of the compensation over the next year was acceptable) and return *God's Penny* to Mydleton. He returned to Watre.

*

Chapter 8

The Grithwoman

The records scattered around the 13th to 15th centuries hold a few cases of women sanctuary seekers, some had committed murders, some were debtors. But one unusual case was a claim to sanctuary at Beverley in 1225. It was the 9th year of Henry III's reign; it was also an important year in the Church calendar. Saint Thomas Aquinas was born that same year and there was a re-issue of the Magna Carta, which is the version that forms the basis of the common law today.

But it was neither murder nor debt, nor the birth of St Thomas, nor even some important provision in Magna Carta, which brought Joan Edwalker to Beverley Minster that June day.

Joan had been married off to Jake when she was 14. Her parents were poor, and both had been ill, they had difficulty in caring for her, the latest of seven children; although apart from Joan only three had survived. There were still too many mouths to feed.

Joan's parents struck a bargain with Jake, who was thirty-five, a widower who needed a young lass to care for him. He agreed to give Joan's parents 10sh. for her; in short Joan's parents sold her for the cost of one cow then, or about £400 today.

Jake was a Butter Badger and they lived in Tickton near Beverley. His job took him all over the county and sometimes even further. He delivered milk and rabbits from farmers to folk in the towns and some manor houses around; he also trapped *mudiewarps* (moles) which he skinned and made into trousers and coats. He commonly carried messages for people since there was no post in those days. During his journeys, he would also keep his ears open for any interesting news of what was happening in the 'outside world'. He was the local 'News Sheet' of those times, though much of his ‹news' was gossip picked up in the pubs he visited on his travels.

His troubles were drinking and gambling and when he had lost, which he did most of the time, or when he was drunk, and this he also was much of the time, he became violent. And beat his wife when he came home. If he did not like the food his wife had prepared, he threw it on the floor. The floor was rushes on hardened earth and cow pat and the food just added the stink in the house. As time passed he grew more vicious and took to beating Joan with his stick, so she had bruises all over her body.

Joan had had two miscarriages and another dies at birth, so she had no children to worry about.

Winter this last year had been bad, the snow had come early, left late and was followed by drought. Come spring the land had dried up and Jake was home; he had lost money at dice and got drunk and had given her an exceptionally rough beating. She had had enough and leaving home couldn't be any worse.

There was no such thing as divorce, nor legal separation, and the constables could not, or would not, do anything to help. Joan had worked out what to do. She waited till Jake was away, donned her coif, a worn wool dress (no underwear, like knickers of course!) put on her reinforced hose and battens, gathered the few small things she treasured, like the copper bangle her mother left her; and with the little money she had saved over the years, she set out for Beverley.

She got to the north door of Beverley Minster and knocked and when the door opened, she said to the monk *"Is it t'place fer san'try?"*. It was clear enough to the priest she was asking for sanctuary, so he took her in. She looked half starved, sick, bedraggled and very dirty so he sent for a nun to take her, clean and feed her and dress her in the usual *grithman's* garb; he would call the coroner to get her story when the nun had finished with her.

The nun returned with her later and told the monk that when she took her clothes off to clean her up, she had seen the most awful cuts and bruises all over her body. She had dressed them as best she could, but the woman was in such poor health that she badly needed rest and food. She had told the nun *"Ah tooken t'rabbits an mudie skins ats wur Jem t'souter"* and asked what she did then she said, *"Ah sell'd em"*. But, said the nun," *A' doo'nt believe 'er"*.

No more did anyone else; but Joan would say no more.

Beverley treated its sanctuary people well and when the Prior heard, he told the Nun to look after her and when she thought she was fit enough only then he would call the coroner.

Some two weeks later, after the nun had reported to the monk that Jane was much better, the monk told the Prior. Then the coroner was called.

When all were assembled with two witnesses from town, Jane confessed to the theft and agreed that she had taken 12 rabbits and had sold them for 15d. That was felony, a hanging offence. There had been no report of a theft nor of anyone looking for her. Jane could not (or would not) tell which souter it was from whom she had taken the rabbits except that his name was Jem, the whole story sounded very unlikely. What was more puzzling was that Jane insisted that she leave the country – abjure the realm in technical language.

With the oath taken by the coroner and recorded by the clerk (which the Prior paid) he explained what would happen if she insisted on leaving the country, to make sure she understood. It would be a dangerous journey and a very uncertain life for her, even if she made it out of the country. He was reluctant to allow her to take this course, but she insisted and said she understood, which the coroner doubted. She would not even hear of any attempt to get her a pardon.

He asked which port she wanted to leave from or would she prefer to go to Scotland. The coroner had to tell her where Scotland was and that to get there, she could take a ship, or she could walk but it was a long way and dangerous; it would take her at least 10 days. She selected Scotland and decided to walk – she was clearly terrified at the thought of going in a boat on the sea.

There was a legal problem about the point of exit from England. It was to be another twelve years before it was settled by a Treaty. The bailiff consulted the Prior, the Prior consulted the Abbot and the Abbot sought advice from the Archbishop (of York), who by chance was on a visit to Beverley staying in his lodgings at the Dings. The Archbishop pronounced that the Meadow of Ba, near Coldstream, was the current border post but, as a concession, since the border country was such a dangerous place, that if Joan were to reach Berwick on the River Tweed that would do.

Joan worked in the kitchens at the minster until it was time to leave; she was in good health and had never been happier. On the appointed day the weather was good, it was time for her to go. There were tears in the eyes of some of the nuns, who were sorry to lose her and feared for her future. Equipped with white robe, wooden cross, a staff and stout battens (as concessions) and some food to start her journey she set off.

Many people in the town had heard of Joan by now, and many were the stories about why she wanted to go away – far away. There was much sympathy for her especially among the women. No one guessed that this was the only way she could think of to escape a disastrous marriage to a brutal drunkard of a husband. Quite a crowd turned out to walk with her to the North Bar of Beverley and a few followed her up the Westwood.

The constable came with her, he would take her as far as the county border where he was supposed to hand her over to another constable from the next county. He did not expect there would be any constable, he was right, there was no constable.

He reminded her to stick to the road and stay no more than two nights at any one place on the journey lest she be branded an outlaw.

So ends Joan's way of achieving a "divorce" from Jake. The adventures of that brave woman in her long mile walk to "freedom" and her experiences of a new life in Scotland remain to be told; but she lived in the memory of Beverley folk for many years, the source of a good story around fires of a winter's night.

Joan clearly was determined that a woman should not be a slave, no wife should allow herself to be treated like Jake had treated her. The sort of life she led, of abuse and drudgery was not uncommon in those days. A century and a half later, and after the black death, there may still have been no divorce laws, but the chances for work improved, especially in the cloth preparation trade, which paid well (though less than for a man). By then women were working with their husbands or on their own. Others were known to travel abroad, like Mary Hogg, or deal in wool, as Emma Earl did in Yorkshire at the end of the 14th century.

The emancipation of women had begun!

*

Chapter 9

Prison Breakout

Prison in middle and medieval times was not commonly used as a method of punishment but of restraint; what we would call today '*remand in custody*' until trial. In those days that could be as much seven years away. The majority of those awaiting trial were not confined at all, the threat of outlawry was enough to ensure they answered the call of the "*horn,*" (note to cap 3) when the judges arrived to hold assizes.

Castle dungeons and the Tower were used too, but more for political reasons, and, in the middle ages for debt. The gaols or any place of confinement were filthy, unhygienic and wet. If you had money or influence, you ate; if you did not, you starved. Few would regard the prospects of acquittal (whether innocent or not) as very high and thus sanctuary offered an option with a chance of life - of some sort.

Escape from a gaol may not have been very difficult, particularly if you had money or valuables with which to bribe the gaoler, but if you did manage to get out you would almost certainly become an outlaw – anyone's "game".

The Thief with Form

John Moore was a thief; he had been a thief since he was eight years old. He must have been a lucky thief, or a good one, to have survived that long.

He was brought up by his mother, who taught him well. His father had been an actor, but an out of work one; he was a vagabond, a vagrant. John's mother brewed ale, poor ale it was, so poor she was put in the pillory once, in the stocks twice and once made to drink her own brew by the scaffold in the market place (which made her ill). She had been beaten up by her customers more than once and was left one-eyed on the last occasion.

For what it was worth John's father was at least a *badged* (licensed) *vagabond,* which may have saved him from being flogged whenever the bailiff or constable felt like it. When he was home, which was not often, he would sit by the embers of the fire of an evening and sleep noisily; drunk if there was anything of his wife's brew which she could not sell left over.

If John Moore's father ever brought anything of value home, it would have been *'lifted'.* Apart from brewing ale his wife made a little money, lawfully, from washing for gentlefolk. Any *'real'* money in that household came from young John's efforts.

. On market days, or fairs, of which there were many in and around Beverley, or when some festival or pageant drew a crowd, young John found pockets to be picked – and he was a deft picker. John was quick-witted and nimble and though suspected by the constables he was too smart to be caught.

John was small for his age, an ideal size to creep through small apertures into homes. A local gang of bigger boys, whose speciality was burglary, recruited him. The houses that they 'did over' with John seemed often to be those belonging to the families for which his mother did the washing! The gang terrorised Beverley and the nearby villages. They specially picked on the weavers in Beverley, who were foreign, mainly Flemish, and unpopular - there was a general dislike for any foreigners, just more for the Flemings, and the constables did not much care what the gang did to them.

John had just turned thirteen when he was caught picking pockets and got a good thrashing. At fourteen he was caught again, this time he was put in the stocks in the Market Place. He left town and for the next two years no one heard of him until he reappeared in Weel, where he robbed an old man of his purse which had a ring and 16sh in it. This time if he was caught, they would hang him.

Someone saw John and raised a hue and cry. He ran. He was young and fast; he soon outran the gathering crowd intent on catching him.

He knew that the only safe place to go was to a church, he knew which church was best; two former members of the gang had been there, they escaped and now were outlaws.

It was a long run to Beverley Minster. But desperation gave him wings and he reached the steps to the north door of Beverley Minster ahead of the mob, which had lost some and gathered others along the way. None of them knew who they were pursuing or why, it was excitement in an otherwise dull day. Just off Flemingate a few vengeful Flemings joined in the chase. The canon on duty let John in and shut the door against the crowd. He rang the Galilee Bell to announce another *grithman* had arrived.

By the time he saw John the Coroner knew who the old man was whom John had robbed. He sent the constable to bring him to the Minster to give evidence. John still had the man's purse with everything in it intact so when he came, John showed him the wallet complete with original contents. The old man identified it and John who confessed, took an oath of fealty to the church and asked the old man to forgive him, assuring him he would do whatever was required of him. The old man had lost nothing and did not want to see the boy hanged so he did forgive him.

Hanging for minor theft, whether a felony or not, and especially of youngsters was not popular with juries. The coroner directed John to be put in the stocks in the market-place and called the executioner to brand him on his right thumb. (There had been a law recently passed that anyone freed after claiming sanctuary should be branded so if he tried it again it would be known).

The local hangman publicly branded John and after he had remained in the stocks five days he was released.

You might think that John would have learned a lesson, at least to be especially careful not to be caught again. However the leader of his gang had other ideas. John was too big now to climb through small windows, but he was nimble with his fingers, was able to melt away into a crowd if need be and a very sharp young man. The leader was a good judge of character and it was not long before John became the leader.

There was an Inn at the bottom of Lathegate near the bullring. It had a bad reputation because it was thought that the landlord was in league with footpads and *Knights of the Road*, later known as highwaymen.

One night John, with some of his gang were in this pub, planning a job on the Goldsmiths Gild building, when two men came across to them, sat down and ordered a jug of ale for them all.

John thought he knew them. One of his own friends whispered to him that they were footpads. After they had all been drinking heavily, one of the two men bent over John and asked him if he would like to help with a job on the Mail Coach leaving the following night from Beverley to York. He told him there was more money and less risk on the road than burglary in town. Greedily, John fell for it and joined them on the venture the next night.

The other two men had horses and told John to get one too. He did, he stole it from the back of one of the stores on Saturday Market in Lathegate. John met the two men at the top of Westwood where they hid in Burton Bushes. They waited for the coach to move slowly up the hill out of Beverley until it reached the top and before the horses could get up any speed, the three of them rode out from the trees up to the coach brandishing pistols. What they did not see in the dark was that the man seated on the front of the coach next to the coachman was an armed soldier, nor that two of the men inside were army officers and also armed. As they reached the coach the soldier shot one of the robbers, another of the robbers wrenched open the door and as he did so one of the officers shot him dead. Another shot struck John's horse, throwing him to the ground.

The soldier leapt off the coach onto John, dragged him to his feet and bound him firmly and then securely fastened him with the luggage on the back of the coach. They took him to York and handed him over to the sheriff to await trial.

On the day of his trial, John was being transferred from the gaol to the court when three men on horseback, some of the same gang he had met in Lathegate, snatched him from the constables and rode away with him. The constables had no horses and they were far away by the time they could be pursued.

John's options were few, he was now an outlaw. Going back on the road did not appeal to him and 'going straight' would never work. He did not want to return to his old gang either. He thought of sanctuary but having been branded, sanctuary would be denied him - if it was noticed. He thought that if he went for sanctuary in a church far away and could keep his hand hidden, he may get away with it. He had heard of Durham, but it was a long walk and very risky. One of the men who rescued him had a donkey which he did not want, so, wrapping himself in a cloak with a hood like a friar, he set off on the back of his donkey.

It took him five days, hiding when the road was busy and only travelling when there were few others on the roads. He made it to Durham Cathedral alright. The monks did not notice the branding, but when he came to confess, he told the truth. What no one had told him was the truth was to be the death of him, '*Lying in wait*', which was what the so-called *Knights of the Road* (or highwaymen) did, was a crime for which sanctuary was not available. The coroner therefore ordered that John be put outside the Durham Cathedral where the sheriff's men awaited him.

He was put in chains and locked up in the gaol. To make sure he did not escape, he was also chained to the wall of his cell. It was a year before he was dragged out, barely able to stand; his trial was quick and he was convicted and sentenced to death. The following day John and 10 others were drawn through the city to the York Tyburn. It was a fine sunny day and there was a big crowd to watch John and his companions being hanged.

*

Chapter 10

Two Women Illustrators and Witchcraft

Juliana Large Sautre and Annicia Lejoin came to York around 1450. Each had a partner, Galfredus and Robert respectively but neither of the couples were married. They all lived together in part of the Norman House off Stonegate.

Both women were the daughters of wealthy London merchants, Juliana's father had been a mercer with a fine house in Hertfordshire as well as his mercery in Cheapside. Juliana had known Caxton from when he was apprenticed to her father. Annicia's father was a wool merchant whose main trade was with Spain and Italy.

Juliana and Annicia were experimenting with woodcut and copperplate engraving producing illustrations for books. Books were being printed in the new presses in York. There was a lingering suspicion among many however that those involved in printing books in English, rather than in Latin or Norman French, were Lollardists at best and witches at the worst. This was particularly so when, as was the case here, they were experimenting with chemicals (alchemy people whispered); in their case of course it was the innocent pursuit of new colours, but that was not what others thought. Barely twenty years earlier a woman, an alchemist, had been burnt at the stake in London for witchcraft.

Things had moved on since the illustrations in such manuscripts as the Luttrell Psalter, and people like Juliana's and Annicia's experiments were resulting in better and different colours. For example to get a ultramarine the best basis was lazurite or the semi-precious lapis lazuli from the <u>Koksha</u> Valley in <u>Afghanistan</u>. Lapis lazuli was (and still is) exported via the Silk Route through the Afghani border into what is now Tajikistan. Galfredus had some years ago been a Franciscan friar and had travelled to parts of the Silk Route and knew the routes the lazurite followed. Other formulae with copper and malachite were also being used, all of which gave off unusual smells.

This laboratory work led to gossip among neighbours. It was whispered that they were casting spells, indulging in witchcraft. One evening Robert coming home found a crowd, of women outside their house. They were ‹calling' (cursing) Juliana and Annicia *"Witches. Burrn 'em"*. One of the women was waving some wooden stick (see note 1). It was unusual to find belief in witchcraft taking such a turn, certainly in York, and in respect of women who were neither in politics nor very old. But this couple were different from the people around and what they were doing was bound to create some mystery, with all the smoke and strange smells. There were tensions between the Franciscan Friary and the Lollards which may have made matters worse, but more likely due to one of the servants in the house having given birth prematurely to a child with a severe, weird, deformity of the face. Annicia had been treating the girl for an ailment for about a week with a decoction of herbs. The midwife attending the birth, who was a vociferous member of the local community, knew this and it was she who spread the rumour that the Devil was in the house.

Robert pushed his way into the house and as it grew dark and as the watch came round the crowd dispersed.

Unfortunately, early the following day the story, and the gossip, of what had happened got to the ears of the Prior and he called the bailiff who then called the sheriff and they decided that, if only for the women's protection they should be taken into custody. In the meantime, Galfredus and Robert had heard of the sheriff's plans and realised what was happening.

This could be dangerous for all of them, particularly the women – though they were innocent of anything, protective custody could well be just another fine name for a nasty place to be put in.

There was a snicket at the back of the property which led to where they kept the horses so the men got some clothes together and told the women to pack and would leave until the furore died down.

They all went through the snicket, mounted the horses and rode as fast as they could towards Beverley so when the constable arrived to take the women he could not find them. He reported to the sheriff. After some enquiries the sheriff became certain of the direction they must have taken and sent two constables on ponies after them. It would certainly be afternoon before they would be able to catch up with them, even if the sheriff was right in his guess as to the direction they had taken.

When they arrived in Beverley, they consulted with the Prior at St Mary's whom they knew. He suggested that to be sure they were not arrested and give time to make some permanent arrangements, the women could seek sanctuary at the Minster. They did so, the Prior of St Mary's accompanying them there to explain the position to one of the canons at the Minster.

Galfredus insisted it would be unsafe for the women to return to York – possibly for some time. Juliana had connections in Brussels and Bruges from her father's day who would probably help them. They could have gone to London or Juliana's home in Hertfordshire, but with both the friars and the sheriff involved in York a claim to sanctuary and travel to Belgium may be the safer course.

They had forty days in which to make their arrangements but before then the coroner had to be called and the women would confess to their experiments and tell of the allegations of witchcraft and the sheriff's warrant to arrest them.

By the time this took place the sheriff's constables had in fact arrived from York and told the coroner what they wanted and why.

The women refused to surrender to the constables and elected to abjure the realm.

Galfredus donned his former friar's tunic and rode back to York to collect all they needed for the journey and arrange for the house to be shut until it could be let.

The coroner had the clerk record the details of the claims and after consultation with the Prior (and a substantial gift – not recorded) nominated Hull as the port to which they should travel to leave the country. Robert meanwhile had already found a ship which would be leaving from Hull and bound for Calais in about 3 weeks' time. The Master of the ship agreed (also for a substantial sum) to take all four of them.

They arrived safely in Calais and proceeded to Bruges where they spent the next eight years executing fine works of illumination of many manuscripts and Breviaries. One of the works was an illustrated manuscript about the King's finest Man O'War of the time.

Galfredus in the meantime arranged for that manuscript to be presented to the King – with a petition that the women be allowed to return to England. The king granted a pardon and they returned to England.

NOTE

1   The stick may have been *Wicken-wood*, which was believed by some to ward off witches.

*

Chapter 11

The Mute

In the 14th and 15th centuries those who were suffering from some obvious disability, such as being blind or lame, would be condemned to a life of beggary. There was little that could be done for such people at that time, nor were there facilities for their care, even minimal attention to the welfare of the disabled had to wait another 100 years.

This story is about a boy called Richard who did have a lucky break. Richard was born in Scorborough between Beverley and Driffield. The time was 1454. The Hundred Years War was just over; it had lasted on and off, from 1337 until 1453 and the international result was England's loss of its lands in France. The results on the home front to the sort of people figuring in these tales was frequently disastrous; the wounded with limbs missing, sores still festering through lack of treatment not to mention those who had lost their minds and the taxes which had crippled many, especially the poor.

Scorborough was a small hamlet populated mostly by tenants and serfs in the employ of the Lord of the Manor (the Hotham family). There were no more than a dozen families; everyone knew everything about everyone. John was born dumb; all he could utter were grunts. There was little understanding or sympathy and he was teased and poked fun at everywhere he went. As he grew older those who did not know treated him as an idiot, or worse a former criminal who had had his tongue cut out as punishment for his crime.

His mother begged the teacher at the school at Lekonfield to take him into his class, she even got John to write on the *horn* (Note 1) to prove he could see, read and even write, which was more than most of the teacher's pupils ever would be able to do. But the teacher still refused to have Richard. His mother comforted herself with the thought that he was not losing much, the teacher was about as dense himself as the bottom end of his own class. What he would miss, by not being at school, was the company of other boys of his age; though he would certainly have to put up with a lot of mockery.

Richard's luck held. He was bright, keen to learn and with lessons from his mother he soon could read and write well. He would still have another hurdle to overcome when he was older. There were few jobs for anyone, and for the disabled there were even fewer opportunities. If he could not find some sort of employment he would end up begging or thieving. Disabled ex-soldiers were a bit better off as beggars since people had sympathy for them. People would think Richard's disablement was due to punishment for some crime he had committed.

Without other boys to play with he developed his own amusements and interests. He had a good eye and became a good footballer and, dumb or not, in most games he was the one to score most of the goals, which made him welcome on any team.

He often watched the former archers, who had served in the wars with the King's armies, at the butts and was envious. He was not big enough for the full six-foot longbow but one of the archers noticed him watching week after week and brought a smaller bow for him to try. He practiced hard and soon got the hang of it. The bowman decided to teach him and the boy quickly became one of the best at the butts. He tried the sling too, and soon became proficient with that too.

As a young lad he got jobs tenting cattle for local farmers, like many other youngsters. One summer night, after he had tethered the animals, and to make sure he would be alerted if any of them tried to move away, he tied a rope onto his belt from their tethering lines. He was awakened by a tug on the rope, thinking it was just one of the animals shifting he tugged back and fell asleep again. However, he was awakened again, this time the pulling continued. He got up quietly and saw three figures, one was quite small and the other two much bigger; they were trying to cut the tethering lines to lead the animals away.

He was one against three but if he lost the cattle, he may lose more than his job. Should he flee or fight? Fight seemed better to him – but how? He had one advantage – the thieves were as slow as the cattle but he could move faster and anywhere. He also had his sling and his bow. He quietly stalked around the thieves and waited for them at the ford. When they got to the water he let fly at the cattle with stones and arrows to stampede them. They trampled through the thieves, who dragged themselves up and fled. Richard got among the cattle and calmed one, and the rest calmed down. He got them together and led them back a different way, watchful in case the thieves returned.

It was getting light by then and all was still in the morning air. He took the cattle to a field behind the farm shut them in and went to tell the farmer what had happened.

By then Richard and the farmer had developed a sort of sign language for communication, with others he wrote on a slate. The farmer was pleased with the boy's honesty and courage and decided to give him a better job.

What no one knew was that a stone from Richard's sling had struck one of the thieves, knocking out an eye. What was worse, and not known either was that the thieves somehow found out where he lived.

The thieves were outlaws and had to be constantly on the move, but the one who lost an eye never forgot nor forgave Richard, nursing his grudge month after month. It was more than a year later, when some of the same band returned to Scorborough, including the one who had lost his eye, found Richard on the farm who was by then a foreman.

The gang waited for the opportunity to take revenge. It came one calm late afternoon in November. Richard was finishing archery practice and was on his way home. The thieves had hidden in some bushes and as John was passing they started to rise up from their hiding place to attack him. Like many who had lost one of their senses had sharpened others – he could hear better than others with all their faculties. He heard the rustle before the thieves broke cover giving him time to notch an arrow and as they emerged he loosed his arrow which struck one of his attackers killing him on the spot; the others ran off.

Richard was left with a dead body; he had killed the one eyed one. Arrows were almost like fingerprints, it was easy to tell who they belonged to, so he could not leave it in the body. Taking his knife he cut the arrow out, wiped it in the grass and put it back in his quiver.

But there was still the body. He went home and told the farmer. He thought the best thing to do was for the farmer to tell the constable. The man he had killed was an outlaw and outlaws could be killed with impunity.

The trouble was no one knew for sure that the dead man was an outlaw, Richard could only tell how he had been attacked and why. He was not keen on going to the constable himself. The only alternative, apart from just burying the body and forgetting all about it was, the farmer said, to claim sanctuary (the closest was Beverley Minster). That would give him the chance to tell his story without the risk of being locked up in Beverley's odious gaol.

This plan seemed to both Richard and the farmer to be the best course so the farmer went off to tell the constable himself, meanwhile Richard went to the Minster and claimed sanctuary. Being dumb he found it difficult to explain what had happened without writing it down. By signs he made the canons understand what he wanted. A slate was brought and he wrote it all down. This surprised the canons: a simple villager able to write?

Neither the farmer nor Richard gave a second thought to the other thieves – they had run off and it was unlikely that would be heard of again - but they were wrong.

The ones who had run off joined up with others and went back to the farm and saw Richard leaving for the church. There were too many people about to do anything to him then so they waited until Richard was inside the church then one of them knocked at the door of the church and when a canon answered the whole band rushed in pushing the canon aside and went for Richard. Vespers were about to begin so all the canons, and the Prior, twelve of them, were assembling in the church and saw the commotion. They confronted this band of ruffians and, seeing they were armed, some of the priests picked up whatever could be used as a weapon and managed to chase them out of the church. In the melee one of the priests was badly hurt and two of the thieves were left senseless on the floor. The rest escaped.

The canon who had opened the door ran to the constable who raised a hue and cry. They soon picked up the trail of the gang and caught up with them at the tollgate at the top of Westwood on the road to Bishop Burton. There was a fight and three of the gang were captured, only one got away.

For breaking sanctuary in this manner the fines would be heavy and whipping was likely but none of those who had been caught had any money and anyway the constable was satisfied they were outlaws. They were all taken to the pillory and there soundly whipped; after that the constable put them in the cells to await the executioner. When he arrived two days later they were hanged on the scaffold in town to the shouts and jeers of the assembled crowd.

The coroner's enquiry easily decided that Richard had acted in self defence, when he killed the one-eyed man, anyway he was an outlaw. There was no reason to put John on trial and he went back to his life on the farm.

*

NOTE

1   The *horn* was an earlier version of the school slate. It sometimes bore the Lord's Prayer. The same expression was also applied when a horn, (the wind instrument) was blown to sound the pending arrival of the Itinerant Justices in Eyre calling those defendants out on bail, as it were, to answer to their indictments; failure to answer rendered them outlaws.

Chapter 12

Death of a Parson

William Harrod was a regular church-goer in the parish of Weighton. He became a churchwarden and was employed by the church to tend the graves and help at funerals for which he was paid 1d for every day he was on duties for the church.

The church needed repairs to the arch at the north door, which had been built in Norman times and was in danger of collapsing. The parson, Richard Hooper arranged for James Thrisk, the Cementarian at Beverley (and Master Mason at Lincoln), to come and repair the stonework. The parson drove a hard bargain with Thrisk who agreed to do the work for 5d a day provided he had someone to help fetching and carrying stone and the scaffolding. The parson persuaded William to give Thrisk whatever help he needed for an extra 1d a day.

The only reason the parson's parsimony paid off lay in the good luck that Thrisk was nearby and his work on St Mary's church in Beverley was held up for a few weeks.

Some of the stone in the arch was disintegrating and needed to be replaced with new stone. The stone Thrisk needed was stone as near to the original as was possible and for that the best quarry was the oolitic limestone at Newbald.

A good sturdy *karre*, or wagon, was needed for the journey, Newbald and back, with loading, would take two days. What was in doubt was whether such a vehicle could get up the narrow track to the church from the roadway, it had to have the right wheelbase.

The carter who had the best waggons was at Rudston. He needed to come to the church to see if he had the right one for the job and whether it could get up to the church. He measured the width of the track, it was 6 foot and the waggon wheels were 5 feet 10 1/2 inches wide; the carter reckoned he could make it, though the hedge may be damaged, and maybe his cart too.

Once the scaffolding was up, Thrisk started dismantling the arch from coping stone down, supporting the stone above with scaffolding. Meanwhile the carter had collected the first load of stone from Newbald which Thrisk inspected before it was unloaded.

Having got some of the blocks down the mason began to cut the new stones to shape, to replace the damaged ones he had removed. Normally a master Mason would have an apprentice to carry out the rough sawing but in this case the parson was so tight with his money that Thrisk did the initial rough sawing himself, as well as the final shaping.

The work William did for the parson was not enough to keep his household fed and warm so he also became the local Butter Badger fetching and carrying messages and getting news, sometimes from as far away as York. What he enjoyed best in that job was passing on news of events outside his local village, usually embellished. He was a natural gossip. But the villagers were happy.

They were not so badly off as they thought; the stories made for good entertainment in pub or home *ower t'owd* fireside of a winter – more exciting by each telling, told and retold, added to every winter night.

There were times, whilst the building was going on, that he had nothing to do for the parson or the Mason so acting as butter badger he took some people's messages to Driffield and York and at the same time got all the latest news.

Whilst in York on one of his trips he paid a visit to a friend, one of the deacons at the Minster. He was always a good source of news. This time the deacon asked him for his help. There was an important letter which the deacon had been asked to get to the parson at Weighton. He asked William if he would take it. William was thinking how much should he ask. The deacon guessed that was what was in William's hesitation, so he offered 6d. William agreed. The letter to the parson was sealed and looked to be official. Being the nosy man he was, he would like to have read the letter before handing it over but could not open it without breaking the seal. Nonetheless in passing news around he pretended he had been given a most important message for the parson and very privately been told what it was about – that parson was in trouble.

His guess was not far off the mark, the Parson had been up to something the Archbishop had heard of and did not like and he was being called to York to face an Inquiry by the Archbishop. Of course this tittle tattle, and who was spreading it soon reached Parson Hooper's ears; he was incensed - as well as being embarrassed that now the whole parish knew; and what more did they know as well?

The parson did not know that it was just a lucky invention on William's part, but even if he had known it would not have improved matters since the story was too near the mark.

The churchyard was a peaceful, quiet spot in the evenings. William often came after the day's work was over to sit and enjoy a pipe. Usually he was alone but sometimes he was joined by a friend.

It was one calm evening, just getting dark when William took a stroll to the cemetery. It was peaceful and he sat on a stone by the edge of a new half-dug grave, lit his pipe and sat half dreaming. The smoke from his pipe was drifting away among the yews. Suddenly his reverie was shattered by a not so gentle tap on his shoulder and a voice. It was the parson who had come up quietly behind William, put his hand on his shoulder and said, *'I want to talk to you William'*.

William leapt up in fright and tumbled backwards into the open grave. As he fell he hit his head on a stone and lay in the hole momentarily stunned.

The parson leant down over the edge of the grave, he thought

William was not hurt so hissed at him "what do you mean *spreading stories about me. I will finish you for that*". William just lay in shock and fright; he did not move. As there was no reaction, the parson began to think that perhaps William may be badly hurt after all – maybe even dead, so he got down into the grave, at which point William came to his senses and thinking that the parson was about to carry out his threat to kill him, he pulled a knife from his belt and struck out wildly, unfortunately the knife went into the parsons throat. There was blood all over him and the parson and in the grave.

The parson was certainly dead; William pushed the body off and clambered out of the grave and vomited. It was dark by then and there was no moon. He dared not go home, with his hands and face and clothes so bloody. If he went to the bailiff and confessed and said it was self-defence no one would believe him and he would almost certainly be hanged, even if he survived the gaol until the next Assizes. If he just went on the run he would be an outlaw. Perhaps if he got out of Yorkshire, where the sheriff's writ did not operate, say across the Humber, he may be safe. But even that was not sure.

When he had last been in Beverley he had heard of a man, Hugh le Orp, who had killed Richard Fallon, a well-known Beverley Keeper, and had claimed sanctuary. He was allowed to leave the country. But Beverley and the Minster at York were too close - the local people could easily find him and fetch him - even out of sanctuary.

The alternative was Durham, which had an important church. He decided on Durham. So that was where he headed; it took him a week. Often he had to hide or travel only by night. There were outlaws all over the wild moors who killed whether you had anything to take or not. Someone might see his bloodstained tunic and until he could wash it all off he feared to be seen close-up by anyone. He looked for some water and found a stream just off the road in some woods and washed off as much as he could.

He was lucky. He saw no one close-by and arrived at Durham without mishap, he banged the big fearsome looking knocker (fig 9), on the north door, was admitted and the Galilee Bell was rung.

Fig 9 Durham Knocker12th century

The coroner and bailiff and whatever witnesses needed were duly summoned. He made his confession, Kyssed the Book. The coroner told William he could stay for thirty-seven days, but after that time he must either leave the church and stand trial or abjure the realm (leave the country). William elected to leave. The coroner designated *Herut eu* (Hartlepool) as the port of departure. At the time that port virtually monopolised shipping within the Durham Bishopric; it was one of the busiest places on that part of the East coast.

The day came when, dressed in a white robe, with bare feet and a wooden cross in his hand, he was escorted to the parish boundary by the constable. There was supposed to be another constable to take him from there, but as usual there was no constable, so, with a farewell the constable turned back.

Sticking to the road he headed for Yarm. As he approached some dense woodland, two ragged ruffians jumped out of the bush, knocked him down, took his white cloak and left him bruised and bloody. He tried to struggle on but soon collapsed, next to a roadside shrine. He rolled onto his side and prayed, how long he lay there he did not know, he lost count of time. He felt a hand gently touch his shoulder, at first he thought *'ootlaws'*, but the touch was too light for anyone like that. He looked up, a nun was bending down over him. The nun was passing by to Guisborough Priory. She got him to his feet and took him to the Priory and left him there. He was taken in, his wounds were tended, he was bathed and fed.

William stayed at the Priory until he was well enough to go on. Reclothed and restored to health, he was all set to leave but meanwhile the monks had tried to find a ship for William, but there were only coastal boats, there were none leaving England, not even to Scotland.

The Prior consulted with the Monastery at Lindisfarne and was satisfied that in such a case as this, as there was no ship, William could claim sanctuary again so eventually a group of friars passing through to Durham took him with them and when they arrived at Durham Cathedral the friars explained what had happened and William claimed sanctuary again.

The coroner explained to William that he could stay for thirty-seven days, in the meantime the Abbot would try to obtain a pardon. If he was not successful William would then either have to stand trial or leave the country. He would be given another port to leave from.

The Judges were on Assize in Durham at that time. The coroner said he could try to arrange a trial quickly if he wished, and to avoid having to be kept in gaol he could remain in the church.

William decided to take his chances in surrendering to trial. His trial soon came up, he pleaded self-defence and was acquitted.

Dare he go home? He had killed the parson and that would soon be known. Anything could happen; someone may take revenge. But he missed his wife and his three children. The promise and comfort of Home outweighed the threats, though he knew he would have a hard time when the facts were out.

*

Chapter 13

Hubert de Burgh Earl of Kent

It has been said that no commoner held as much influence as did de Burgh until such men as Cardinal Wolsey and Thomas Cromwell appeared in the reign of Henry VIII.

The Earl of Kent was the Chief Justiciar in the reign of King John and present at the signing of the first Magna Carta. Earlier he had fought in the Crusades and in France, where he also held prominent positions. By the time he became Chief Justiciar he was also a very wealthy man: it was that which was his eventual undoing.

He remained prominent after King John died, in the reign of Henry III, King John's son, but his fortunes soon took a downward turn. He was not as impregnable as he may have thought, or hoped. What follows describes the period when his fortunes were at a low ebb. Most of the events are drawn from the pen of the well-known medieval historian Matthew Paris, but even then gaps and uncertainties abound.

The des Roches family, in particular Bishop des Roches, was an arch enemy of de Burgh and following King Henry's major defeat in France the Bishop told the King about a very large sum of money which, so he claimed, belonged to the State, had been stolen by de Burgh and handed to the Knights Templar for safe keeping. The King either believed this story or welcomed an opportunity to embarrass the Templars, get his hand on some money and at the same time compromise de Burgh.

He demanded that the money be retrieved from the Templars and handed over to him – de Burgh refused.

Unsurprisingly de Burgh was afraid of what the King may do to him and he therefore sought sanctuary in Merton Priory, well known at the time and where Thomas A'Becket had once studied (it is a Sainsbury's now!).

The King was no respecter of the privilege of sanctuary, where money or his position were concerned, nor is there any evidence that he feared eternal damnation if he ignored its guarantees of the safety of sanctuary. On this occasion he ignored them. He directed the Mayor of London to force the Earl out of the Priory. De Burgh, on hearing what was to happen laid himself against the high altar. He no doubt knew very well that if the Mayor and his officers took him from there forcibly they ran the risk of excommunication. Whether to avoid the mayor's excommunication or for other political reasons, or both, the King countermanded his order.

De Burgh then betook himself off, cross and host in hand, to South Weld, a chapel of ease in Brentwood. That move did him no good. He was seized, mounted on a horse with his legs tied beneath the animal's belly, and ridden off to the Tower of London.

The Bishop of London and his clergy told the King that all those involved in this abduction, which was the heinous breach of the privilege of the church's sanctuary, would be excommunicated.

Once again the King publicly appeared to relent, and de Burgh was taken from the Tower back into sanctuary at South Weld. Privately he told the sheriffs of Hertford and Essex to mount a guard round the chapel and not to allow any food to be taken into the chapel. To reinforce those instructions, and make escape more difficult, a ditch was dug around the chapel. De Burgh therefore had the choice of starving or or allowing himself to be returned to the Tower; he chose the latter and was taken back to the tower in chains.

What happened next is not recorded but de Burgh must have made some part payment to the King for he was then sent to the castle of Devizes. Having been deposited there he made yet another escape by jumping into the castle moat and thence going to a nearby church – no doubt with a little help from friends. He was pursued and even though he was prostrate before the altar with the cross in his hand he was violently dragged out and taken him back to the castle.

This challenge to the authority of the church was such that the Bishop of Sarum took himself off to the castle. First he tried to obtain de Burgh's release by persuasion, when that failed and the governor of the castle refused to hand de Burgh over to be returned to sanctuary, the Bishop promptly excommunicated the governor and his accomplices in this outrage. The Bishop of Sarum and the Bishop of London, and other prelates, urged the King to restore de Burgh to sanctuary; yet again, he did, so, but true to his accustomed duplicity, the King directed a guard be set around the church to prevent any food being brought in for him.

De Burgh was nothing if not persistent, for a troop of armed men, assembled by his supporters, rescued him from the church and took him to Wales where he stayed the rest of his days and died there peacefully.

Whether he paid over the rest of any money he may have owed, and if not where it went are mysteries for another day – by then the King had bigger problems on his hand, and it should be remembered that whatever his faults, King Henry has a record of being a competent administrator and had re-enacted provisions of Magna Carta. He does not have the same reputation for the pettiness and cruelty of his father.

*

80

NOTE

1   Contemporary sources for this account may be found in *Chronica Majora* RS vol III Matthew Paris. Also *The Fall of Hubert de Burgh*, Carpenter D Journal of British Studies Vol. 19/2 (Spring, 1980), pp. 1-17 CUP is the interesting product of much research into the life of de Burgh

2   Wikipedia: "In 1229 Henry unjustly blamed him for the failure of an expedition against France, and in 1231 the justiciar's bitterest enemy, Peter des Roches, returned from a crusade and won the king's favour. Henry then dismissed Hubert (July 1232) and imprisoned him on charges of treason. In 1234 he was pardoned and reconciled with the king.

Chapter 14

A Manuscript to Murder for

William and John Salvan were both Esquires, Sir John Heghfield, George Walker and John Hunt were rich; gentlemen of such means that they did not need to work and Walker and Hunt were wool merchants and ship owners living in Hull.

All five were keen collectors of rare manuscripts and books. Heghfield, in his travels to France and Italy had already acquired several including one of the copies of Virgil's Bucolics and Aeneid, and the others had acquired some manuscripts and one had a Breviary by Jensen.

They met regularly, at each other's houses, to discuss different aspects of this topic which had begun several centuries earlier and continued to produce beautiful manuscripts; each had a particular manuscript which they wanted to acquire – at any price. There were also some new works by English artists which engaged their attention. One was by a woman whom they heard had, until quite recently, been working in York, but was now in Bruges.

With the contacts they had made on their travels they were in a good position to look out for bargains and, by sharing their experiences, they were able to help each other.

In one of their meetings in the hot summer of 1477 they had heard of Henry Hardwycke who lived in Beverley, and who was said to have acquired a particularly beautiful and very rare Breviary, believed to have been made in Venice in the previous century. They were interested to see this; Walker went further, he made it clear that he was determined to have it. The others rather suspected that he was not too particular about how he got it, either. After some enquiries they found that Hardwycke lived in Beverley at number 15 Flemingate.

Travel to Flanders had been severely interrupted because of the extensive flooding that year so they spent most of their time at home. In December 1477 the group met again and decided to approach Hardwycke to see if he did have the manuscript which George wanted so badly, and if so whether he would sell it.

Heghfield and George Walker were delegated to go to call on him. They travelled to Beverley. They knocked at the door of number 15 Flemingate which was opened by a maid, of whom they enquired if Mr Hardwycke was at home. She replied that he was in town and should be back directly, she asked them if they would care to come in and wait – they did so. Whilst waiting they were able to see some of Hardwycke's collections of art, particularly some of the illuminated manuscripts and magnificent carpets, some of which they could identify as coming from Khotan in Samarkand by the knots used. They were impressed and thought that the man clearly had taste.

At that time Beverley was encouraging the arts, not the least because of the very recent introduction of printing, though it would be another 25 or so years before Beverley itself had its first printing press.

Shortly after Mr Hardwycke arrived and they had introduced themselves to each other, they started to discuss common interests over an excellent Madeira. Eventually Heghfield broached the purpose of their visit. Hardwycke hedged, neither admitting nor denying he had this very same manuscript but confirming his interest in such works of art as a collector.

Walker was particularly upset at being unable to get a sight of the object of their desire; not only to see its condition but to have evidence that it was genuine. He believed that Hardwycke did have it but there were many forgeries and copies of such works around and until he could see it he would not know if it was genuine. They had to leave therefore no further forward - just suspicious.

Walker set his mind to find some other way to see it, if Hardwycke did have it.

Having returned to Hull, a meeting of all five was called to discuss what was to be the next step. The Salvans and John Hunt were keen to drop it, at least for now, but Heghfield and George Walker wanted to pursue it and suggested that at least they needed to be sure he possessed it and if so that it was genuine – if possible with some provenance. The only way to achieve this would be to gain entry to the house while Hardwycke was out, George felt he would be able to form an opinion as to whether it was genuine or not. The others were not persuaded that this was sensible, if caught their reputations at the least would be gone and if prosecuted they could expect to be sent to gaol. George thought that unlikely, because if they were caught they would be able to buy Hardwycke off.

There was no agreement and George was left simmering; he was not to be put off. He had contacts among many in the wool and cloth trade in Beverley, particularly among the Flemish, who he was sure would help him – for a fee.

Times were harder for them now, with the decrease in importance of the wool trade in the town, and the hostility which there had always been toward foreigners.

This attitude extended beyond those from another country, even to those from other towns, they were called aliens. Many Flemings bore grudges and George knew the 'underworld' well, he had not been involved in the smuggling trade for years without learning where to look for help. He soon found two men who would welcome the chance to take revenge on Hardwycke for being cheated by him more than once, but they came at a price.

The Flemings were instructed to keep a watch on the man and when he was going to be away they were to tell George. With a few pence in the maid's pocket, it would be easy to get into Hardwycke's house.

The opportunity soon cropped up. George told Heghfield only and asked him if he wanted to come so they could look at the manuscript if it was there. He agreed, provided the Flemings did not come into the house and were able to see him. They chose a dark night, with mist off the marshy parts of the town and the promise of heavy rain. The maid had left the back door open as arranged and had gone out. Heghfield and George searched the house; eventually they found the Manuscript hidden in a drawer and, with it, a letter. They examined the Manuscript as carefully as they could by candlelight and both were reasonably satisfied that it was the original. But was the letter useful provenance?

It was and it was not. It was from the man, who on Hardwycke's instructions, had taken the manuscript from the cathedral in Rheims and would hand it over to Hardwycke on receipt of the rest of his fee. They were to meet by the front door of the church of the Holy Sepulchre in Paris to complete this transaction. There was no date on the letter.

If they took either the Manuscript or the letter Hardwycke could hardly report its loss to the sheriff but he could guess who had taken it and exact revenge. George suggested they should leave both and blackmail him into selling it cheaply. Heghfield believed that the letter showed it was stolen but lent credibility to its genuineness; they needed the letter. After much discussion it was agreed to leave both where they were.

George's Flemish friends reported a week later that Hardwycke had returned. The five of them met and reported what had happened. It was agreed that a letter should be sent to Hardwycke inviting him to meet them by the cucking-stool in the marketplace in Beverley the following Saturday, a market day when it would be bustling with people and very noisy. Heghfield was to approach Hardwycke alone, the others were to wait in the crowds nearby.

When they met, Heghfield said to Hardwycke, ‹*We know you have the Manuscript we talked about. We want to buy it*' Hardwycke at first refused but then said, *'I want £100 in Angel's'* (gold nobles), to which Heghfield replied, *'That is far too much let's get Domenico Villani to put a value on it, I know the partner in the bank'*. Of course Hardwycke could never allow anyone, especially someone like Villani, an Italian, to know he had a stolen Venetian masterpiece. He tried to bargain *'I will take £75'* to which Heghfield responded ›*I will pay £20 and no more, if you don't like it I will speak to Domenico Villani when I am in London this week and tell him about this manuscript and where it is'* (Note 1).

Hardwycke, was sure that Heghfield, was bluffing, but he could not take the chance of Villani learning that he had the stolen manuscript, it would be his ruin at best and more likely his death. But he could do nothing where they were then so he said, ‹*Very well, come to my house on Monday, come alone and bring £20'*.

Heghfield reported to the others what had happened and Walker and Heghfield were the only ones who could be said to be happy. The others were apprehensive at the way in which the whole matter had been handled. Heghfield was simply suspicious of Hardwycke and said he would not go alone nor would he go unarmed.

Monday came and, despite their misgivings, all five went to Beverley. They dismounted from their carriage further down the road and walked towards 15 Flemingate. Heghfield was several paces in front. It was dark, they could not see the small group of men near Hardwycke's front door until Heghfield was almost there. There were only two men, one with a sword, the other with a club. Heghfield just had time to draw his sword, he shouted and ran the first man through, the second man struck at Heghfield with his club, but caused little damage, George went at that man and knocked him to the ground. They all then barged into the house and were met by Hardwycke with a loaded pistol which he discharged wounding John Salvan, Heghfield drove his sword into Hardwycke killing him instantly.

Chapter 15

The Two Recruits

Edward III had recently returned from a campaign against the Scots. He was about to embark on another campaign, this time in France and he needed more recruits.

Two archers, who had been training regularly at the butts in Beverley had become well known, winning many competitions at which they made money in prizes. They were using the longbow, England's wonder weapon, five to six feet long, a weapon which was used with phenomenal success at Crécy nine years later.

They were outside the Standard Inn in Beverley discussing the merits of joining the King's army for France. There were others drinking outside the pub, they were arguing, if incoherently, about something. One of the archers asked someone in the crowd what it was about and was told they were talking about the press-gang going around the villages near Beverley forcing men, even lads as young as thirteen, to join the army and the navy. The pressed men had no choice whether it was army or navy, nor which part of the army they would be sent to. No one wanted to serve with men they did not know, or who were from other parts of the country. Some argued for joining voluntarily before being pressed, others said they would hide. Someone in the crowd shouted, *"there's gold to be 'ad when we beat t' French"*. The two archers listened.

The idea of joining up, and doing so voluntarily as archers, and with one of Hotham's local contingent, seemed better than risking being impressed (forcibly enlisted). It was true that there was always booty to be had if the battles were won and one survived. You come home get a wife, maybe a farm and settle down. The two archers mused *'aye an put yur feeat oop by t'fire'*. So they decided to join Lord Hotham and set off, a bit unsteadily, to find his steward, bent on joining up. They knew they were good archers and sure Lord Hotham would be glad to have them.

On their way, however, there was a brawl outside the Blue Bell in which a constable was there trying to calm things down and establish order, but not having much success. In trying to get past this crowd of drunken people, and themselves still unsteady, accidentally bumped into the constable and knocked him over, when he fell he hit his head on a stone and there was blood on the path. The rest of the brawlers seeing him lying there quickly disappeared, leaving the two archers standing, fixed to the sport in confusion – but they sobered up. Spying another constable, who clearly had seen them in the light from the alehouse, they fled down Wood Lane and across the market. They were not thinking where they were going but found themselves at the bottom of Highgate near the north door of Beverley Minster.

The constable, with a posse, was not far away so the two archers banged on the church door shouting to be admitted. The priest on duty let them in. They were not articulate about exactly what they wanted, but from the bits of the story which tumbled out it sounded like a claim to sanctuary. The crowd at the door and the constable's voice could be heard which confirmed the priest's conclusion.

The Galilee Bell was rung and one of the canons let the constable in to find out from him what had happened. Having heard his version of events the canon directed the constable to return with the coroner in the morning. They got their *grithman's* garb which they were told to put on and left them to sleep.

The next day the coroner and the clerk and bailiff were called. Both archers told their story and confessed, but claimed it was an accident. They took the oath, Kyssed the Book. The coroner explained they could either be tried or they would have to leave the country unless a pardon was forthcoming. They elected to leave the country since that way it seemed that they would still be able to join the army.

Two weeks passed, during which time the sister of one of the archers had found out where her brother was and came to see him. He asked her to get their bows and arrows and bring them to the church. What they had not realised was that they would not be allowed to carry them when they left sanctuary.

The two archers made the most of the church's hospitality but were careful not to wander too far from the church, there was always a risk of abduction from sanctuary, whatever the penalties those committing such a breach may be faced with. The real threat was the press gang.

A day or two later, as they were sitting on a stone by the open church door they saw a group of armed men heading towards the Minster. They guessed it was a Press Gang and fled into the church threw themselves on the *friðstol;* they should have been safe there - they were not. The press gang burst in, grabbed them and took them out of the church.

It was not only the press gang who came, it was the sheriff as well who, with his own men had come to arrest the archers and take them off to prison to await trial. The Prior sent a message to the Bishop complaining bitterly of this breach and demanding the sheriff, his men, and the constables all be excommunicated and the rest of the men whipped. The Prior also insisted that the sheriff return the archers to the church immediately.

However Lord Fauconberg (not Lord Hotham as the men had hoped) was short of the number of archers required of him by the King. One of his bailiffs was in Beverley at the time, recruiting for the Earl's force and heard of the two archers. He reported back to

Lord Fauconberg telling him where they were and what the sheriff was trying to do. The Earl sent a knight and two soldiers to take them out of the sheriff's custody and bring them to him. When the knight arrived he only got one archer, since there had been a scuffle outside the church whilst the two archers were being taken away from the church, and one was so badly hurt and soon died.

The sheriff was in due course excommunicated along with those who participated in the snatch from sanctuary – and at the very altar. He petitioned the King and the Archbishop of York, and with Lord Fauconberg's support the excommunications were set aside, but the sheriff was heavily fined and his men were whipped.

The archer who survived went to France as he wished, and a good deal more safely and comfortably than it would have been if he had been 'abjured the realm'.

A few years later a visitor to Lekonfield found an ex-archer farming there with a young wife and two very active young lads.

*

Chapter 16

The Chaplain and the Lost Rents

By 1519, when this case arose, sanctuary had got such a bad name being so frequently abused and having, it was generally thought, outlived its usefulness had been severely limited by the law so fewer and fewer claims are found in the records. The entire privilege of sanctuary was to be abolished just over a 100 years later. Nonetheless there are still claims to be found, if one looks hard enough, and this was one of them.

One major reason for someone to claim sanctuary was nothing more than the fear of what may happen, justified or not, for some minor transgression or fear of damnation. Sometimes it was fear of a lynch mob at one's heels, not necessarily for any wrong the victim had done. However in Thomas the chaplain's case, the fear was what his employer, the Earl of Derby might in his anger, do to him.

Thomas Ley was the chaplain to the Earl of Derby. The Earl had extensive lands in the Midlands and in Lancashire, and even the odd tenant in North Yorkshire. One of Thomas' jobs was to collect the rents from the Earl's tenants and any debts due to him.

Thomas was a thin, nervous little man, with a pronounced tic when agitated – which he easily was. His movements reminded one of a pigeon, quick and jerky. He never looked you in the eye and when he did, he spoke in a whisper. In contrast, his wife was large, with a voice you could hear from one end of the village to the other, and when she sang in church – which she loved to do - her sonorous notes made even the old stones put their fingers in their ears!

Thomas was terrified of most people in authority – especially the Earl, his wife was in awe of none, much less the Earl who dreaded every encounter with her. But Thomas was honest and efficient, and he cost the Earl very little – until this one day.

Thomas had come from his last collection of a debt in the sparsely inhabited wolds and moors of North Yorkshire. He traveled on a twelve-hand pony, though to do his work more quickly and in more comfort, a horse would have been better. He did not think he deserved such a luxury as a horse, anyway it would be at least sixteen hands and that was a terrifying thought.

The debt he had to collect was a long journey from Carlisle and, though it was still late summer and warm, it was almost dark by the time he neared Carlisle. The dark made Thomas shiver with fright, he imagined being robbed or murdered, not unlikely in the wild and lonely parts of North Yorkshire. Fortunately there was an Inn nearby where he had stayed some years ago, so he stopped to enquire if there was room for him that night. There was, said the innkeeper but he would have to share the room with another (as was common when an Inn was full). Thomas just wanted food and a bed and agreed to take what was offered.

He took his supper and some watery ale. He was carrying £58, which was a lot of money to be carrying alone, especially in these parts of the country; it would have been wiser to have at least two armed guards. Thomas was never given or even offered anything like that level of protection and did not dare to ask for it.

After he had eaten, having taken what he thought to be enough care to hide his bag of rents, he went to bed and soon fell fast asleep.

The next morning, he was up early but his roommate had already gone. Thomas checked the bag of money was still where he had put it the night before. It was, he did not open it then, just hefted it, it clinked, was heavy and seemed OK. He had breakfast, saddled his pony and was about to put the bag into his saddle bag when he thought he would check inside it. He opened it. It was full of stones! He nearly had a heart attack! Recovering his breath he looked inside more closely; it was just stones and a few coins at the bottom. He counted the coins; they came to £13.6sh.8d He sat down and *greeted*, (wept), in sheer desperation; he prayed and went outside and was sick. What was he to do? His master would, at best, sack him, more likely he would be beaten or gaoled, even hanged for theft. What was he to say to his wife?

Fear drove this otherwise indecisive man, to reach a firm decision. He knew all about sanctuary so that was what he would do, he would claim sanctuary. Others in the past had done it when their debts were too much for them so why not him. It was not so easy these days, only a few churches were safe; it would have to be either Durham or Beverley. He decided to head for Beverley. It took him two days' hard riding, stopping one night in an old, deserted hut. When he arrived at the Minster he had to knock hard and call out to make the duty priest to hear and let him in.

The next day the Prior sent for the coroner, bailiff and clerk and after their fees had been paid, he confessed to what had happened, took the oath of fealty to the church and *Kyssed* the Book.

The coroner was unsure what to do with Thomas. He was clearly just a poor unfortunate soul, terrified of what the Earl would do to him, but he was no criminal, not even a debtor. He called on the Prior to discuss with him what should be done. The prior sent a message to the Earl of Derby to tell him where Thomas was and ask if he should he send him back to the Earl.

In his letter the Prior explained Thomas' story and told the Earl that both he and the coroner were satisfied that the man was honest and that the theft from him may have been due to carelessness.

He sealed it, and when he had heard from the Earl that Thomas should be sent back to him, he gave the letter to him, had him provisioned for the journey home, and gave him in charge of an itinerant friar, who was travelling the same route.

Thomas was still very uneasy; would he end up in a debtor's prison? Or be flogged and dismissed? He would never get another living. His companion the friar, who had once been a court minstrel and carried his lute with him, played and sang ballads, as well as reciting interminable poems, hour after hour after hour, especially at matins, lauds and prime. At least it took his mind off what he thought awaited him when he got home.

When they did get back home he went to meet the first of his fears – his wife and the friar went to hand the letter to the Earl or his Steward; he then continued his journey.

To Thomas' astonishment she swept him up into her very ample bosom, as though she had feared he may never return, and she did have some doubts about this, bathed away all the dust dirt from his travel, put clean clothes on him, fed him and listened to his story.

The Earl sent for Thomas. His fears reawakened; he was trembling. His wife insisted on being with him when he went to the Earl; whatever else she may sometimes be she was loyal to her husband and would defend her nervous 'little pigeon' as she called him, with all she had (and it was a good deal).

Bolstered by his wife's presence, but still trembling, he sought out the Earl. What he did not know was that the friar had handed him the letter already. The friar used all his charm as a minstrel and played an air for the Earl's wife - so the atmosphere was cheerful when Thomas and his wife arrived. Having read the letter he bid Thomas speak but he was dumb with fear, so his wife spoke up and said, ‹ *Yer Lordship robbers 'at token t'money'*. To Thomas, the Earl said *"speak ter t. chaplain:* ‹after much mumbling and fidgeting and wringing of hands, the tale spilled out in a rush of semi coherent sentences which the Earl cut short with a loud bark, his wife put her hand on his arm so he simply told the chaplain to get out; he would knock £10 off his stipend.

Thomas did get out – fast - not believing he was still all in one piece.

Chapter 17

"Longbeard" and a Breach of Sanctuary

If you travelled back in your time machine one factor of life which you would recognise in whatever country and in whatever century you landed in was tax. And where there is tax you will also find protesters protesting. In Longbeard's day the rich and powerful devised ways to pass the taxes onto the poor, the poor usually could not pay but even if they could, and did pay up, they knew the money would be wasted in some useless way, either by a king in a pointless war, or appropriated by the local lord on fine clothes and sumptuous living.

Today one remembers the Poll Tax and the riots in March 1989 and in 1990 – *"Bollocks to the Poll Tax"* wrote Colin Revolting (yes, his name) 30 years later. But to show that history teaches nothing to some, one of the many taxes being demanded was also a Poll Tax in 1377; this triggered protest and revolt, though it is doubtful if it was the tax itself which was the chief cause of the riots, but it contributed to their intensity and to the aftermath.

However, go back a century, to 1296 to be precise. This is when Longbeard entered the picture.

The claim to sanctuary this time was not in Beverley, nor Durham, nor even in the North, but in London, at St Mary-le-Bow. The claim at this church demonstrates the distinction between the general and the special kinds of sanctuary described in the Introduction. And it also tells us how the powerful prelates, men of God, supposedly, looked after their interests and when they did they showed up some of the cracks in the church's claim to the inviolability of the protection of sanctuary.

William Longbeard was the nickname for a man with the finer name of Fitz Osbert. Historians of the day said he had a semblance of education and an impressive gift of the gab. His detractors called him a rabble rouser, and that is what he was. He made a great deal of noise in the city over yet another tax by the King to finance yet another, useless Crusade. None of them succeeded, and thousands died.

Longbeard had himself been a Crusader but returned penniless and his 'good' family gave him no help. But he raised, and then led, a so-called political party which, remarkably, attracted 50,000 adherents. He played the nobility against the King by protesting that though the tax was intended to be spread fairly between rich and poor, the main burden of the liability to pay the tax was passed on to the poor, the nobility avoiding their fair share; this, he claimed, was a demonstration of disloyalty to the King.

There were riots, and the nobility got a force together to capture Longbeard, but his own supporters massed around him to prevent his capture and in the fight that followed one of the nobility's forces was struck from his horse and broke his neck. Who knocked him off his horse has never been discovered. One story is that Longbeard was the culprit; for this he was arrested, tried, and condemned to death. He escaped, but whilst getting away he killed a guard, even though he claimed that he did not kill anyone and the nobility had cooked this story up, he still sought sanctuary.

St Mary le Bow was a bad choice of sanctuary. Longbeard could not produce any evidence that St Mary le Bow enjoyed any privilege of sanctuary (it was not a special sanctuary). What was worse, the church was part of the Archbishop of Canterbury's See and the

Archbishop, Hubert Walker, was also the Kings Justiciar and a particular enemy of Longbeard.

Whilst in sanctuary the Prior offered Longbeard the opportunity (on the Archbishop's instructions) to save his life if he submitted to ecclesiastical law. Longbeard knew that if he left the church he was a dead man. Even if he was not dead, under ecclesiastical law he was likely to be confined in uncomfortable surroundings and silenced. He refused to leave.

He was not offered the chance of abjuring the realm, clearly his enemies were bent on silencing him completely. His supporters had all drifted off by then.

The Archbishop had Longbeard at his mercy. With another Justice and armed men the church was surrounded. What happened next is not clear. There are two versions of what took place next, one was that Longbeard was smoked out, which was the view the Monks took. The other view was that he caused a fire in the church. What the monks were at loggerheads with the Archbishop about was the breaking of sanctuary by the Archbishop himself. It was years before that feud was forgotten.

There was little sympathy for Longbeard's cause, except among the poorer citizenry of London, it was easy therefore for the Archbishop to destroy his image and prevent martyrdom. It was put about, no doubt by the Archbishop, that Longbeard had confessed to having asked for Satan's help, and, what was much worse, he had had sex with his concubine in the church *(polluting the church with semen'*; it was that which above all else put him outside the protection of the church.

The collection of a large quantity of iron tools intended to smash houses and fortifications were, it was claimed, found among his belongings when his house was searched which did nothing for his cause, in fact it sealed his fate.

Whatever story about the lead up to Longbeard's fate, his end is clear. He was tried (again), convicted and sentenced to a traitor's death. He was drawn to the scaffold at Tyburn on wattle fencing, hanged by the neck, but before his struggles were over at the end of the rope, he was cut open and his entrails burned before him. Thereafter his body was cut into four parts and his head put atop a pike on London Bridge.

That fearsome price was paid by many others over the middle ages seeking the freedom to protest, to speak out against oppression. Rights, which in this country, are taken for granted today; rights which need a zealous watch for the tenuous claims to the need for their restriction.

Chapter 18

The Missing Rector of Wycliffe

For some centuries, the peaceful little parish of Ovington and Wycliffe, near Durham, had one small church situated in the village of Wycliffe. Except for one of its vicars or rectors especially, it was a parish of little interest to the outside world.

That rector was John Wycliffe. His history is well known. At that time the Church ruled from Rome and was still a powerful force in the country. Wycliffe was questioning the wealth of the Church, the place of the Priests and transubstantiation. He is credited with arranging, if not writing, some of the first translations of the Bible into the English language. Before this the Bible was in Latin; they were also expensive and not every church had one. Even where there was a Bible, few, even among the clergy, could read it.

To him is also attributed the early birth of Protestantism, his later followers being, derogatorily, named *Lollards* and in the next century his body was exhumed and burnt for heresy.

It was Chancellor Cromwell, in the reign of Henry VIII, who vowed to make the new Bible available in English in every church in the country. The Bible was to become open to all, not just the clergy.

About a century after Wycliffe's death, the then future Bishop of Durham, John Sherwood became the rector at Wycliffe church. In his rise from humble beginnings, with the support of Neville, the

Archbishop of York, he was appointed Bishop of Durham and then Ambassador to Rome.

The rector(or vicar) who followed after Sherwood was Sir Rowland Mewburn or Mebbum, whose family was well known in the area and whose name can be found in records down to the present day – but is missing from the board in the church which lists all the rectors.

This tale explains why.

It would not be an unreasonable guess that Sherwood and Mewburn and earlier rectors after Wycliffe were followers of the Papal church and were appointed in reaction to the move toward Protestantism which Wycliffe was seen to herald.

Since Wycliffe's day there must have been rumblings among the parishioners who now had better access to the Bible in their own language and began to see the errors sometimes preached in the past.

The peace in that little parish of Wycliffe and Ovington was broken by the violent death of a parishioner.

Early in 1482 Sir Robert Mewburn, then the rector, summoned one of his more notable parishioners, a gentleman named Robert Mansfield of Ovington, to see him at the church. On arrival the rector challenged Robert Mansfield for his failure to pay tithes, and furthermore for encouraging his family and other parishioners to do likewise.

Mansfield answered Mewburn, saying the Church was doing little for the parish with their money. He, the rector, had denied them the use of the English Bibles and used their tithes for his own benefit.

This was a serious allegation and if pursued could damage the rector's continued occupation of very comfortable living. The rector lost his temper and moved toward Mansfield raising his stick (as before it was his sword stick). Mansfield, thinking he was about to be attacked, struck the rector's stick with his own walking stick. The force of the blow was such that the sword broke through its wooden sheath. Mansfield's own impetus carried him onto the point of the bare steel which penetrated his heart, as the record holds 'he died incontinently" (instantly).

The news of the pardon to Mewburn eventually reached James Mansfield, Robert's close kinsman. This angered James who thought it most unfair since Mewburn did not seek sanctuary nor did he make amends or even apologise to Roberts' family.

For over a year anger consumed him so that finally he could bear it no longer. He resolved that he must avenge Robert's death.

Sir Robert Mewburn, the rector was granted a pardon, by King Edward IV which must have been before April 1483 - when that King died. Thereafter there was conflict over the young King's Protectorship and it seems unlikely that a pardon would have been obtained so quickly. Who interceded for him and why, and why the King (or his Protector) should pardon a man who had not claimed sanctuary, nor stood trial for any offence remains a mystery.

Some said that the canons obtained the pardon, but why should they be involved? Given the conflict between the Papacy and growing Protestantism in the country, coupled with the North of England's history of rebellion, one may hazard a guess that it was the then Archbishop Rotherham of York, known for his ambition and questionable tactics, who wanted to keep a Papal Prelate in the living.

On Sunday January 25, 1485, James Mansfield, one of Robert's kinsmen, along with his family attended morning service at Wycliffe church; they were not regular churchgoers to that church, but James wanted to be sure that Mewburn was there and maybe confront him. But he said nothing.

The next day James, together with some other relatives, went to speak with Mewburn at the vicarage. They do not seem to have had any plan of what steps to take. He was not only the rector but a knight and a man with much influence in the county.

It was late afternoon when they arrived at the vicarage. The door was answered by a servant who told the callers that the rector was at the church but should be home soon. He invited them into the house to wait for him. James declined to stay and they all started to walk back over the field between the house and the church. As they did so the Reverend Mewburn, his black robe flying around him, was striding across the field towards them.

As he drew near, close by a small copse, James called Mewburn, who answered, asking what he wanted. James replied, *'Lord Mewburn I would have word with you please. About my kinsmen's death'.* Mewburn replied, *'It was an accident, I feared for my life.'* *'But you are free, you have not made any offer of compensation, nor expressed a single word of remorse to his kinsmen. We want some settlement from you.'* retorted James.

James and his companions had drawn close to the rector. James raised his stick and pointed it at Mewburn, starting to speak, but before he could utter a word Mewburn drew the sword from its cover and said, *'Do not threaten me you shall have nothing'*, waving his blade in James's face. There was a bill (a wallych or Welsh) billhook lodged in a log nearby, no doubt being used for copsing. James grabbed it and struck out intending to knock the rector's sword away, but the bill slid down the blade and struck the vicar in the chest giving him, in the words of the record *'a mortal wound, from which he died'.*

Two days later James went to Durham Cathedral, banged on the fearsome-looking knocker on the north door, was admitted and claimed sanctuary.

The records show that the coroner called before him the present rector of Kellow, Roger Morland, and Nicholas Dixon as witnesses to James' oath that he had killed Sir Rowland Mewburn outside the church of Wycliffe on 26 January just past with a *wallych bill*, an unusual type of copsing tool in this part of the country.

As was common in Durham, James (not a monk) was instructed to ring the Galilee Bell himself to announce his claim to sanctuary.

The coroner gave James a choice, either he must abjure the realm(leave the country), Seaham being the port of departure and not return without a pardon from the king or he must leave the church after thirty-seven days and stand trial for murder. James was reluctant to stand trial. Even in the unlikely event of his acquittal, any period in gaol, however short, could leave him crippled for life. At least he was likely to be allowed to await trial at home until the *"horn"* sounded the arrival of the judges at which he must answer for trial, or be branded an outlaw.

James considered he was avenging the death of his kinsman. His killer had not been punished; no apology or *wergild* (compensation) had been offered. Compensation paid to kinsmen for a death had generally gone out of fashion after the causing of the death of another had become a felony; but it was a way of keeping peace within small, and often isolated communities.

The clerk failed to record James' occupation, as he should have done. He was, in fact, a metal worker and was a respected member of the Durham Gild of Metalworkers.

A Burgess of the Gild heard of James' plight and went to see a canon at the Cathedral with whom he played the organ and told him James' story.

James' grandfather had arrived in Durham as a Pilgrim from Canterbury, some three hundred tortuous miles away. With him he brought a St Thomas Pilgrim Badge beautifully crafted from pewter. He also had an Ampulla he had bought at Lincoln on his way. He himself was a pewterer and he had met a local woman whom he married and decided to stay on in Durham.

He went on to produce local badges such as the St Cuthbert's Badge, which he made from lead and whistles too. All these were bought by pilgrims who were passing through on pilgrimages or setting out on a pilgrimage from Durham.

He was well known and had given part of the money he earned to the Cathedral. He died and Robert took over the business. When he was murdered James took his place and expanded the business to the use of copper and even brass. One product was the Walsingham Whistle which was made in the shape of a cockerel, and another, much admired by ladies, was a *Forget-me-Not*, the flower for love and remembrance - like rosemary for Hamlet's Ophelia). The flower was made of ivory with a blue topaz chip set in the centre. It was considered a work of art and was expensive. The Burgess explained how the church and the country benefited from his workmanship and what an asset James was. Noone wished to lose him.

The canon consulted with the Bishop, the Bishop consulted the sheriff, who conferred with the coroner; all agreed that if James consented to remaining in the town and gave half of his profits to the church he could stay, officially as a ‹slave of the church›.

So that was how James ended his days.

But the tale would not go away: local folk to this day will tell you that if you pass the church at the dead of night, when the wind whistles through the yew trees in the churchyard, you can hear the rustle of a gown of silk as the ghost of that *'incontinent'* priest's unhappy and unshriven soul still haunts Gretaside.

Chapter 19

The Burgesses of Beverley

The Burgess appears during the reign of King Edward the Confessor, and during William the First's reign. What this title meant is unclear except that then, it seems to have indicated that a burgess was a trader or merchant who carried on his occupation under the protection of a Patron. Wikipedia suggests it meant someone who sought shelter, perhaps in a 'burgh'. Susan Reynolds, in her Introduction to the *History of English Medieval Towns* gives an insight into what 'made' a burgess; she recognises that the term was not set in stone and observes that *'Already, however, controversies about consultation were contributing to the need for a closer definition of who was a full citizen or burgess of his town and therefore eligible to be consulted'* - in elections.

She refers to 'lesser burgesses' and follows with *'It was stated then there were three ways of becoming free: by patrimony, for those lawfully born in the city (which it is maintained by this author could not be removed); by apprenticeship and by redemption'* (ie paying for it). Of the first there are no records until later and became generally linked to membership of a gild.

What it was not, was a family name taken by some of those who fled persecution of the Huguenots to England and came from Bruges; that was not to happen for another five hundred years.

The word *burgess* is derived from the Latin word *Burgus* which means a fortress or a walled place, in English a Burgh, hence a Borough. Perhaps the unexpressed spirit of the burgess was some form of protection. This, the burgesses in the tale which follows may have been the root of a burgess in whatever way it was enjoyed.

When Beverley became a Borough, and its inhabitants were given the right to own their own land in the town, that give the male denizens, or inhabitants the right to be addressed as burgess. In a class-conscious society which existed at the time such a title was much coveted. With it went several privileges and exemptions, though it did impose a duty to contribute to the ransom of a king when needed.

The first grant of a right to own land outright, and therefore inheritable and freely transferable, an early form of freehold, was in 1114 by King Henry I; the land was called a *Burgage* (note 1) and the grant referred to burgesses. Bishop Thurstan confirmed the grant to Beverley of its own form of local government with 12 Keepers or 'governor. Thus Beverley became a burgh, the Borough of Beverley.

The burgess who fell into the patrimony category were male inhabitants of the Borough who owned a burgage, and it seems must have been born in the borough. They were free; they were burgesses by birthright. At what point it was required that their fathers should also be burgesses and in a lawful marriage (not a concubinage) is unclear. But society was in a constant state of change and adaptation, at every level including burgesses (note 2).

Beverley grew wealthier, the two markets yielded good returns to the closed shop of the merchants, traders and craftsmen in their Gilds. Both the king and the Archbishopric of York (he had a place in Saturday Market – the Ding) derived benefit from the markets in fees for permissions to trade, and the multiple tolls (see the Glossary for some examples).

By the end of the twelfth century the town had become the 11th largest town in England. Trade was such, mainly from the wool trade that the main gilds needed a place to meet. Recognising this, and no doubt receiving a handsome payment, Henry gave Beverley a *Hanshus* or Gildhall,

In 1263, King Henry III exempted Beverley Burgesses from arrest for debt and gave them the right to come and go as they pleased, throughout the county – including York – without having to pay all those tolls. These were privileges attached to being a burgess. There were duties too, of course. If there was a violent uprising in town, or attacks on the Borough from outside, all burgesses were required to help put down the first, and rally to the town's defence in the second.

Some of the changes to life, among those who needed a stall, or place to display their wares had set them up outside the town, beyond the gates. The disadvantage to this was there was little or no protection from attack, robbery, or violence, which were real risks with no police force, The stalls were set up close to the gate to the town so the marketeers could, if they were quick enough, run through the gate into town for safety.

All this changed with the grant of the right to burgages. Hitherto a form of slavery with serfs and vassalage existed but now, in effect, men could own land, they were free – emancipated (Note 3). The merchants and traders could abandon their stalls outside the town and trade from their property in town, First as a place to trade, but soon they built on the land and it was a place to live in as well, downstairs for business, upstairs as a home.

Trade and wealth brought other, less attractive changes. According to Susan Reynolds, in her book *The History of English Medieval Towns* different classes and hierarchies, grew up in the thirteenth century.

The Gilds got a grip on trades in the towns; aliens, and those without a licence were excluded. But the gilds needed officers, a chairman, at one point called Alderman. Maybe members of the wealthier gilds just adopted the title of burgess and it was accepted, but in the majority of cases the title of burgess went with appointment. Likewise the government of the borough would have needed officials, and maybe the title of burgess went with the appointment.

In the case of burgesses who acquired the title of burgess by their appointment or office if they lost the office they would also lose the title.

Logically if it was the circumstances of their birth which gave them the title of burgess, neither gild nor Keeper could take it away; they could not change the facts

Some historians suggest that it was the burgesses who were at the top of the power pile in a borough (note 6). Though that was not the case in Scarborough in 1258, when some *mediocres* or middling class of people, (were they the' lesser burgesses' as well?) imposed fair trading practices on the town's burgesses who were abusing their office or trade.

By the latter part of the 14th century the town oligarchy consisted of the major gild members (burgesses no doubt) and the Keepers. The Keepers became so oppressive with fines and high taxes and puritanical laws, such as banning dicing (though ignored) that they became unpopular. This led to a revolt. In the meantime all the major posts in both government of the town and gild came to be occupied by the same people.

Who was a burgess has the ring of Humpty Dumpty in Alice in Wonderland about it; his view was '*When I use a word, 'it means just what I choose it to mean — neither more nor less.*'

From *Grithman* to Burgess

The Peasant's Revolt had been over nearly 50 years, but the in-fighting in the local government of Beverley, which was then at its peak was still smoldering on (Note 4) when a fisherman, Mr William Gelle, (Note 5) appeared on the scene seeking appointment as a burgess in Beverley. Where he came from or why he wanted to be a burgess is one mystery. Why two eminent members of the local gentry took up his cause and wrote on his behalf to the Keepers in Beverley is another mystery. But they did.

Sir Henry Bromflete joined forces with Mr John Ellerker in writing a letter to the Keepers in 1429 requesting that William Gelle be made a burgess.

Sir Henry was only about 17 at the time, but he was to become Lord Vescy, Ambassador to France and sheriff for Yorkshire, like his father, and John Ellerker,'s father was a Serjeant at Law and his wife was Lady Elizabeth Hotham from a well-known local family.

Mr Gelle does not appear to have told anyone of his rather tawdry past; he had, at some time, claimed sanctuary and thus was known as a *grithman*

The Keepers were clearly minded to grant Gelle's request, until they heard that he was a *grithman*, whereupon they refused to help; they went further, and decreed –

> *'that no such person who had committed an offence against the common people or against the peace of the Lord King henceforth carry on his person a knife or dagger, except with blunted points, nor any club or sword in the Town of Beverley on pain of forfeiture of the same to the archbishop and forfeiture of his Burgessship … of the town of Beverley for ever'.*

They also demanded an oath be taken by anyone aspiring to become a burgess. The form of the oath was ' … *and I am fre and no Grythman.*'

But why, despite such an explicit ruling against a *grithman* holding office, and having his burgess-ship forfeited, did they change their minds? Mr Gelle's request to be made a burgess was granted!

Whether the Keepers had gone so far as to extract an oath from Gelle is not mentioned, it is unlikely that they would have done so, since it was a matter of record that he had claimed sanctuary and was a *grithman*; he was therefore not '*fre*'. The Keepers knew that.

Was the position 'once a grithman always a grithman'? Were there different categories of *grithman*? There are no records of a *grithman* ceasing to be a *grithman*. But the Keepers' change of mind in regard to Gelle could be explained if there were different categories, or degrees. The oath the Keepers required was of a grithman who had committed '*an offence against the common people or against the peace of the Lord King*'. If Gelle had claimed sanctuary for a debt that would neither be an offence against the common people nor (usually) a breach of the peace. Sanctuary was a method used to escape creditors, even if only for breathing space and was an early form of bankruptcy. The Keepers, mostly merchants, never knew when they themselves would need such a breathing space, so would not wish to extend any exclusion that far.

All that is known of Mr Gelle's background is that he was a fisherman. It can be presumed that he was not a *burgess* by birth; perhaps a license to sell his fish was in some way tied up with his request to be made a burgess.

An Alderman claims sanctuary.

By 1380 there was a mini coup; a group forced a change in the method of local government. There were outcries against the tyranny of those governing the town which led to a revolt by the inhabitants. The immediate outcome can be seen in what follows.

There is an example of a well-known figure in Beverley politics in the late fourteenth and early fifteenth centuries who did claim sanctuary and who was restored to his former status – Richard de Midelton.

There were squabbles in the Council chamber which had started in 1380; the country was in an uproar over the Poll Tax in 1381 and there were riots in several parts of the land. Whilst there were pockets of rebellion in the county, it was the domestic squabble which occupied most thoughts, and actions, in Beverley. What is more, they continued long after the Poll tax riots were over, spilling on into the fifteenth century. Richard de Midleton was at the heart of what was a struggle for power. Domestic it may have been, but it came to the King's ears and he sought to put an end to it. These events, and more, are faithfully recorded in *The Memorials of Beverley Minster* and *The Beverley Town Riots* (note 4).

Richard de Midelton was an Alderman in Beverley. He had been appointed, along with two chamberlains, by a group of 'malcontents' to govern the town in place of the Keepers. They had taken the Common Seal and other valuables. This came to the ears of the King who reprimanded the usurpers (Richard and his fellow chamberlain) for changing their form of government. The disorder continued and during the summer of 1380 Richard and others forcibly extracted bonds; one such Bond was a promise to pay Richard de Midelton £200, conditional on the payer (Adam Coppandale, a member of a local Beverley family) abiding by a judgment due to be given by Archbishop Alexander of York. Many of the other malcontents took flight but Richard de Midelton did not flee, and when he heard a rumour that the Archbishop's decision would be unfavourable to him and was considering action against him, felt it wise to find a haven for the time being. He therefore claimed sanctuary at the Minster.

The Abbot knew him and knew that his term as Alderman was soon to expire so, in the usual manner he called the coroner clerk and bailiff, as well as two witnesses. However, before the arrival of the coroner, Richard had two visitors. One was one of the other chamberlains serving with him, Henry Newark, who tried to persuade him not to claim sanctuary but, if he really was in fear, simply to leave town until the dust had settled.

The other visitor was Thomas de Manby, the new Alderman elect. He related a story, which he had heard, that Richard had nothing to fear from York; and he thought that the Archbishop was soon to deliver his judgment. But Thomas also said that there were enemies in town whom, he had heard, were making threats to Richard's life.

Richard was in a dilemma. If he claimed sanctuary, he would be unlikely to be able ever to stand for any office again. He may even lose the position he held as a burgess if his enemies had anything to do with it. *'The threats were not idle ones – he should take them seriously,'* added Thomas.

By the time the coroner arrived Richard had made up his mind to go ahead with the claim to the privilege of sanctuary, he was not a felon nor had he committed an offence against the people, though perhaps there had been breaches of the peace. He did not think it was likely he would be exiled. It was a fear of what other people may do to him from which he needed protection.

His oath was taken and with all the procedures pertaining to such a claim complete, the coroner told him that he had forty days in which either to leave the sanctuary of the church or remain as a servant of the church for life. The abbot assured him however that in the meantime he would seek a pardon from the King if that was necessary.

The option to remain a servant of the church was not as bad as it sounded, since the practice in Beverley allowed him free run of the town and all being well, he may be able to persuade a future board of Keepers or his gild to allow him to return to his trade as a mercer. Anyway by then the danger from the threats may be over.

He handed over his outer garments including his Alderman's hood and was given the *Grithman's* robe; being a gentleman the Abbot allocated him a room where he could stay.

At the expiration of his forty-day respite there was still no decision by the Archbishop But there was a deluge of writs and petitions to the King, especially over extorted bonds. This led to a summons to appear before the King. Manby was supposed to take him to the King together with the bond itself, but Richard could not be found, at the church or anywhere else. In fact, he had gone to Durham to seek sanctuary again there.

Over the following year the writs and restitutions continued. Fortunately for Richard all the extorted bonds had been found and surrendered and a pardon for Richard had been obtained from the King.

According to Thomas de Manby the threats to Richard's life had not gone away and he should beware if he returned to Beverley.

Richard had a kinsman Sir John (who had been the clerk) and who was prepared to look after his interests. He now felt it was safe to return to Beverley.

But de Manby was right. Not long after his return, in 1385 Richard was violently assaulted by John de Erghun. He survived the attack but Erghun killed another man in the affray. Erghun was tried for murder but was acquitted.

The troubles in the town continued, but Richard de Midelton did manage to re-establish himself as a mercer and presumably was accepted back into his Gild. No mention is made about being a burgess.

*

NOTES

1   Burgage. See note 2 Introduction.

2   It was not until 1460 that there was a general prohibition against a *grithman,* becoming a burgess; again this could not, without specific legislation, affect a burgess by birth.

3   Some make a distinction between burgesses and freemen in the town. There does not appear to be any authority for this, nor does the dictionary make this distinction.

4   Thanks to the Transactions of the Royal Historical Society. The Beverley Town Riots and citations Beverley Minster Reg 13,f.77r & f.92v

5   Victoria County History - Yorkshire A History of the County of York East Riding: Volume 6, the Borough and Liberties of Beverley is the source of Gelle's tale but not the commentaries upon it.

6   The Burgess Lists which survive (early 19th century) contain surprisingly few names, but they do show where each burgess lived, in each ward, clearly over their businesses and on the burgage with strong resemblance to the measurements revealed in medieval times. One hundred years later those lists seem more like voter's rolls; and by then aliens, both men and women, were being freely admitted as what amounted to burgess, even if they did not use that term of themselves.

*

Chapter 20

Crime, Abuse of Office, and Robin Hood.

Historical programmes on TV today – Starkey, Schama, Lucy Worsley – present us with fascinating stories of the great and the good, or the bad. History at school is frequently the memorising of the dates when Kings ruled, what they achieved, or what they lost, which King cut whose head off, or disemboweled at Tyburn.

The tales told earlier are intended to show how some of those who sought sanctuary lived and died. Why, by misfortune or intent, they needed to seek shelter from injustice – and *from* justice.

This chapter illustrates what every butter badger would have been retailing, and embroidering, in his village in the 15th century. Similar events hit the headlines almost every day today.

<u>Crime</u>

The mafioso of that century was the family of the Folvilles of Ashby-Folville in Leicestershire, and their associates in crime between 1326 and 1347. The family members were seven brothers and their mother. Their lives are strewn with notorious murders, kidnapping, extortion and sundry other felonies. In 1340 at least two of the brothers, and the mother, were involved in the murder of

Baron Bellers (of the Exchequer Court). The leader of the gang was Eustace, but the actual assassin was Ralph la Zouche.

Their lives of vicious crime contained arrest and escapes from gaol, some through pardons from the King, others by deportation to the wars in France. Gaol-breaks were followed by claims to sanctuary of which there is one specific report of the brother Richard. After he had sought sanctuary the sheriff, not to be deterred from getting and hanging Richard Folville, sent his officers to the church to haul him out forcibly. Having done just that he did not wait to have him tried but without delay he had Robert's head struck off while still within sight of the church.

The Folvilles were but one example of a gang of criminals operating throughout the country at the time, the members of which were drawn from both nobility and outlaws. There is even a folksong from Scarborough about the state of law at the time called '*The Fisher's Ballad*'.

Surprisingly some of those gangs were acclaimed "Robin Hoods" in popular opinion. A letter written by the Parson of Huntington, near York, refers to "*Robins,*" '*plying in about the vicarage at Burton Agnes in East Yorkshire.*'

The stories of Robin Hood are born out of a dream by the poor and vulnerable that someone will ride to relieve their grinding poverty and avenge the wrongs done to them.

Sir Richard of Loxley from Nottinghamshire did apparently exist. He was said to be the Robin Hood of the 1330s. The public clothed *him* as The *Robin o' t'Woods*' of their dreams seeking to right wrongs by the sheriff and robbing the rich to give to the poor (Note 1).

Due to the weight of business on the administration in a country in a "*War State*" (the constant wars, the Crusades, in France and trouble between England and Scotland) the responsibility for keeping law and order in the counties was devolved upon local justice and sheriffs. The sporadic arrival of the King's justices - often

119

only every seven years, was unpopular, but local justice quicker but often too quick and unjust.

There had been extensive complaints about the administration of justice, abuse of office and, possibly more important to Edward, the extensive unchecked poaching of his deer in Sherwood, particularly in Nottingham. The King therefore went there to hold his Court personally. Whilst there, that very same Sir Richard of Loxley, so history assures us, was the King's own *valet de chambre*!

Abuse of Office

The official court Rolls of the 14th century reveal the extent of the abuse of office at the time, lending support to that part of the tales of Robin Hood concerning the sheriff of Nottingham, among many other sheriffs, bailiffs, and reeves. It illustrates the abysmal state of good order and the administration of justice in the country and the place for the existence of the privilege of sanctuary as an immediate and secure place of shelter. Though in that same century there were judges such as Martin de Pateshull and William de Raleigh whom Bracton regards as exceptional judges.

What follows is taken from the special Eyre Rolls (1258 to 1260) when Hugh Bigod was Chief Justiciar, and another fine judge of that century, which leaves us in no doubt about the extent of abuse.

The ability of officials, such as the bailiff, or even the sheriff, to intimidate those around him and make or unmake the tranquillity and harmony of the village, was no small thing and the stories illustrate what could, and did, happen in that century.

There were five women, out of a total of 18 complainants, both villeins and tenants, reflecting a cross-section of the village's inhabitants, brought actions against three bailiffs who farmed a royal manor belonging to King Henry III. The jury accepted the evidence of the complainants and added a few other infractions from their own knowledge! The bailiffs were gaoled and forfeited their right to hold the manor which would be quite a loss to them.

On 20 August 1258 William de Rushton, a bailiff of Woodstock, together with others faced charges of torture, resulting in death; the unjust hanging of a pregnant girl; hunting in a Kings Park and assault and burglary. De Rushton and one of his sub-bailiffs were convicted, gaoled and their possessions were confiscated but the torturer, another bailiff Robert Togod, was hanged.

That was not an end to de Rushton's troubles. Along with his bullyboys he entered homes, beat up their occupiers, trashed and removed their belongings. What is more, they even put some in gaol, and the conditions in most prisons have been described in earlier tales. For other misdeeds damages, which ran from 20 to 100 shillings were claimed from William de Rushton and his three sub-bailiffs. William lost custody of the manor, which was worth £40 a year; and for good measure he was put in gaol as well.

In December 1259 John of Ashen, who was a Royal bailiff and another bailiff John Baldwin each ran the same racket of accepting bribes to exempt people from jury service; the first was put in gaol and the second fined.

But it was not only bailiffs who were guilty of such abuse, sheriffs were also guilty. The sheriff of Northampton, Hugh of Manneby had been wont to assault innocent people and in 1225 four of his men, attacked and badly injured Richard of Glaston, who as a sanctuary man, was on the road to Dover to take ship away from England, having been banished from the country. Richard was first imprisoned in the cellar of Manneby's own home and later was taken to hospital. In effect he was an outlaw and therefore had little recourse to justice, but he was keeping to the rules, and this attack was therefore a breach of the privilege of sanctuary and a breach of the King's Peace.

Justice Bigod heard Richard's complaint and Manneby and his accomplices were put in gaol; but he did not suspend Richard's journey to Dover – if he recovered. For this offence the sheriff, along with his men, was imprisoned and warned that if Richard died, he would be tried for murder. Manneby was very lucky, according to

Matthew Paris not to have been hanged but, as things turned out, Manneby claimed benefit of clergy (Note 2) and handed over to the Bishop of Lincoln.

In September 1258 the sheriff of Lincolnshire was amerced (fined) for delaying the hearing of a writ of nuisance for seventeen months, contrary to Magna Carta 1225. Yet another sheriff Williams of Lashborough of Gloucestershire, took a woman's cow, put it to work and when it calved kept the calf notwithstanding writs ordering the cows release. For these and related offences he was fined half a mark and gaoled (Note 2).

*

NOTES

1 Alexander McCall Smith relates a modern, and readily understandable, example of a sort of modern version perhaps of the Robin Hood approach in, *Joy, and Light Bus Company* where Mma Potokwani knowingly accepts illegally obtained or "dirty" money which she could use for the benefit of her orphaned children. (p 55).

2 Special Eyre Rolls of Hugh Bigod 12358-1260 esp Vol I 2021 published by the Selden Society and edited by Andrew H Hershey – with his permission.

Chapter 21

The Church's Role: Sanctuary and Asylum

'Auschwitz, Bosnia, and the Destruction of the World Trade Centre revealed the darkness of the human heart. Today we are living in a tragic world, where, as the Greeks knew, there can be no simple answers, the genre of tragedy demands that we learn to see things from other people's points of view'.

The Great Transformation
p. 476 Armstrong K 2006

Sanctuary, in the form described in earlier pages of the Medieval times and Middle Ages could not survive in an ever-developing world. An improved administration of justice, the loss of the forceful backing of the church of Rome, as well as its abuse, inevitably led to its abolition. But its soul, as it were, the protection from injustice, the concepts of mercy and compassion, live on.

Despite the abolition by Henry VIII in 1540, of sanctuary in all churches bar eight, (note 1) which must have included that privilege in Minster at Beverley, it was followed by the dissolution of the Chantries in the first years of the reign of his (9-year-old) son

Edward VI in 1548 (note 2) (nothing but legalized theft) it did linger on until it was abolished by James I in 1624.

Despite this 'final solution', sanctuary emerged out of the ashes three hundred and fifty years later. Not up to medieval standards of safety, but still in churches, first in Europe and North America, and later in the UK.

Viraj Mendis, a young man from Sri Lanka, arrived in England in 1973 to study. He had a visa for two years. When that time was up he did not ask to stay longer, but neither did he go home. He became "an illegal".

Whatever else he was, he was inventive. First he claimed social security, though he had no right to it; he got away with it for several years. When, at last, he was rumbled in 1984, the Home Office had him arrested. He was released, but the Home Office was preparing to deport him. To avoid this he found a girl to marry (at a price), the Home Office branded it a *"Marriage of Convenience"* but did nothing for another two years until he was handed a Deportation Order to Sri Lanka.

This was where sanctuary came in. Father John Methuen, Anglican Minister of the Ascension Church in Manchester, after consultation with members of the local community, agreed to allow him to stay in the church. Mencius, speaking, long ago for all religions, and none, writes that *'If religion is to bring light to our broken world, we need, to go in search of the lost heart, the spirit of compassion that lies at the core of all our traditions'*.

The church did not challenge the abolition of the privilege of sanctuary nor claim any powers to resist the right of the State to enter a church and remove Mendis by force, if necessary. It considered the Christian had a duty to try to preserve that spirit of compassion, fill a gap in the laws, give the breathing space to allow for further reflection, even if there was no lynch mob howling for blood at his heels.

Nevertheless Mendis did achieve a temporary pause to see if the Home Office could be persuaded to change its mind, but it would not But it still did not do anything for another two years.

In 1989 there was a sudden flurry of activity, the police arrived at the Church of Ascension in full force, armed with pickaxes and sledgehammers as if to confront a rebellion of armed insurgents,. They dramatically, and with great show, 'overcame' Viraj Mendis, removed him from the church to prison and thereafter deported him to Sri Lanka - he was back in Europe within six months.

The church did not try to fine or excommunicate the police or the Home Secretary as they may well have done half a millennium earlier.

There were very few other illegals or asylum seekers who followed in Mendis' footsteps in the UK (note 3). Though a Methodist minister in Glasgow in 1989 did allow a young Ghanaian student, who was facing deportation, to remain in the church pending a decision in her case, before the Court of Session in Edinburgh. The minister was careful to make it clear that he was not relying on 'sanctuary' for support, because he did not think such a thing existed anymore.

North America's story is different. It was more outspoken and it was linked up to local communities as well as the churches, in attempts to resist deportations. In this context the on-going action and debate in Canada, and the United States is enlightening.

There was debate in the New York Times and there is much academic literature, some of which is mentioned in the Bibliography. The Ryerson Centre for Immigration and Settlement in Canada prepared some working papers (2017/1 and 2020/5) based on research which they had carried out which give a good insight into how sanctuary is interpreted and operated in Toronto and why. Canada's humanitarian tradition of concern for those who have sustained human rights abuses resulting in displacement from their homes is an important factor in the work done in this field (notes 4 & 5).

Toronto declared itself a City of Refuge. It had identified that, asylum seekers and their families who were illegal, and therefore undocumented suffered needlessly from many unseen deprivations. They have, for example little access to police help when targeted by anyone for anything, and they have inadequate access to care facilities; especially for the young and the old. They can be given unhygienic accommodation which may continue for long periods in inclement weather before being attended to.

The cities and states in North America which have declared themselves as Sanctuary places have done so to help restore dignity and basic care to the vulnerable. This is a message for others - protect your borders but do so with compassion and understanding (note above 4).

Some brief extracts of a Question-and-Answer debate in Canada went thus:

Q: What drives leaders and the state to keep this *relic* (of sanctuary alive today?

A: 1. As Christians we are called to speak out for peace and support the principles of sanctuary. It is good to hear churches in Britain, Ukraine and elsewhere offering prayers and opening their doors. Every church can be a church of sanctuary.

2. Churches only intervene where the government is itself in danger of breaching international law and fail to design a refugee determination system with adequate procedural safeguards to prevent refugees from being deported to face persecution.

Professor James Hathaway (the *academic* father of refugee law literature) reaffirms the international law which prohibits the removal of *anyone who* meets the refugee definition to face persecution. That is NOT just those whom the state recognise as such. This seems to be a conundrum, but it is aimed at the shortcomings of many refugee determination systems.

The churches and communities in the UK did eventually start to go down the same route as North America. The movement *Sanctuary Cities* started by the Methodist Reverend Inderjit Bhogal has had a positive response from some towns and cities as he said *"With our global economic standing we can express better hospitality. Instead of spending heavily on keeping people out of the UK, we should be investing in building cultures of welcome, hospitality and sanctuary'.*

In the ancient Greek City States asylum was generous in their welcome of foreigners with open arms. Whether such hospitality would have survived the numbers displaced today one cannot know.

Today, in Greece there is a movement, which is worth mention, even if it is neither sanctuary nor asylum-seeker oriented - it could be said to be Utopian. This initiative has led to self-established organizations which are *not* doing charity work, *nor* helping people in need out of compassion or mercy but are directing their activities within a framework of a perceived global struggle to smash racial discriminations and economic exploitation. This they aim to achieve by abolishing the conditions which give birth to wars and racism and consequently to refugees. Their view is that refugee-status determination systems are, and always will be, inadequate. It is the root cause of refugee displacement which must be addressed.

Peter King, both judge and ordained Minister puts both the dilemma and the call to us all well:

> *"There remains the great Christian Tradition of hospitality towards the stranger set against the hard nut of immigration control to protect our borders against the unauthorised stranger. How to safeguard the benefits and interests of the citizen whilst treating the needy with fairness and compassion ... More and more the Church is challenged to speak out ... Afghanistan, Syria and the Ukraine have reminded us of the moral imperative to help our neighbour in time of need and amend our understanding of what it is to be a refugee.*

Jan Egelund, Director General of the Norwegian Refugee Council rings a major alarm bell when he claims that the asylum system of Europe is deficient and requires an overhaul. If the willingness of countries, globally, to remain unreceptive to principles of the Refugee Convention continues, and most likely worsens, he is right. What is necessary is a global, not just regional, harmonisation of border policies, idealistic as this may seem. Even then, without something of the order of the Greek movement related above there will always be refugees.

The entire system of refugee protection as envisaged by the Refugee Convention is built upon the notion of solidarity, and the sharing of responsibilities to an extent consistent with a country's own economic and domestic conditions. This is nothing new; St Paul, writing to the Galatians, admonishes *'Live creatively...reach out to those who are oppressed. ... share their burdens'.*

To summarise: national attitudes toward control of the movement of people across their borders have had a poor record of success even when they became draconian. They lead to unnecessary suffering by the vulnerable – intentionally, and unintentionally. Globally, when cooperation should be the watchword, there is conflict and confrontation; when the focus should be on burden sharing, there is only myopic self-interest. On the domestic scene this situation inevitably leads to the absence of harmony between church and state, where cooperation would be humane and in the long run should be cheaper and more effective.

The most recent policies and legislation highlight the gulf between views on control of borders between states as well as between differences within a country (Note 6)

The story of sanctuary is not dead, it continues to resonate every day in the lives of those 'whose background is forced displacement' in every part of the world (Note 8).

***

NOTES

1   *Managing Change in the English Reformation: the 1548 dissolution of the Chantries etc.*
    Gill S M

2   1540 32 Hen. 8 c 12 An Act concerning Sanctuaries, Privileges of Churches and
    Church-yards. abolished all bar 8 sanctuaries, Edw 6 (1548 c. 7 abolished chantries.

3   Mendis was not the only one then or later; Eva Mensah, Salema Begum, the
    Ogunwobi family were others.

4   Professor Simeon deals briefly with Canada's 'humanitarian approach' in chapter 7
    pp 213-217 of *Migrants and the Courts: A Century of Trial and Error.*

5   See bibliography: The New Underground Railroad. *This Ground is Holy: Church
    Sanctuary and Central American Refugees.* Church of Sanctuary (project supported
    by Churches Together in Britain and Ireland).

6   The UNHCR (updated) Observations on the UK Nationality and Borders Bill (now
    an Act) in January 2022 explains how far it infringes the UK's obligations under the
    Refugee Convention and Protocol. Especially rendering asylum seekers 'illegal' and
    proposing to remove some to other countries: such an attempt failed in 1986.

7   Painting of Jovcho Savov on the cover which echoes Picasso's painting of Guernica
    from the Spanish Civil War.

*

APPENDIX

AÍGYPTOS BORDER AGENCY!
Joseph Jacobson+2
Date of Birth: Unknown
Our Ref: Date:
Nationality: Judean
Your Ref:

Dear Mr Jacobson,

Disputed REASONS FOR REFUSAL

- You have applied for asylum in Aígyptos and asked to be recognised as a refugee under the Convention Relating to the Status of Refugees on the basis that it would be contrary to the country's obligations under the Convention for you to be removed from or required to leave. You claim you have a well-founded fear of persecution in Judah. A person is a refugee where, owing to a well-founded fear of being persecuted for reasons of race, religion, nationality, membership of a particular social group or political opinion, that person is outside the country of his nationality and is unable and, or owing to such a fear, is unwilling to avail himself of the protection of that country; or who, not having a nationality and being outside the country of his former habitual residence, is unable, or owing to such a fear, is unwilling to return to it and is not excluded from the protection of the Convention.

- Your application has not been considered by the Secretary of State personally, but by an official acting on his behalf.
- Consideration has also been given as to whether or not you qualify for a grant of humanitarian protection in accordance with paragraph 339C of the Immigration Rules. A person will be granted humanitarian protection if the Secretary of State is satisfied that:
  - substantial grounds have been shown for believing the person concerned, if the person returned to the country of return, would face a real risk of suffering serious harm and is unable, or, owing to such risk, unwilling to avail him or herself of the protection of that country; and
  - the person is not excluded from the grant of Humanitarian Protection.
- Consideration has also been given to whether you may be eligible for a grant of limited leave to enter or remain in the country in accordance with the published Home Office asylum policy instruction on discretionary leave.
- Your claim for asylum is based upon a fear that if returned you would face mistreatment due to your membership of a particular social group. Your claim for humanitarian protection is based upon your fear that if returned you would face a real risk of unlawful killing and torture or inhuman or degrading treatment or punishment in the country of return.

Basis of Claim

- You claim:
- You claim to come from Nazareth and to have travelled with your partner, Mary, to Bethlehem to register in response to

a decree of Caesar Augustus organising a census. While you were there your partner gave birth. You say that you are not the father of the child.

- You claim that you were warned in a dream to take the child and his mother and escape to Egypt because the local ruler in Bethlehem, King Herod, was intent on searching for the child to kill him.

<u>Consideration of Claim</u>

- Your claim has been considered, but for the reasons given below it has been concluded that you do not qualify for asylum or humanitarian protection. It has also been concluded for the reasons given below that you do not qualify for limited leave to enter or remain in the country in accordance with any published policy on discretionary leave.
- Your claim to have been warned by an angel in a dream is found to be incredible. You made no attempt to identify the angel when interviewed. Your explanation that you responded to the angel's directions because you had been told by another angel on an earlier occasion to stand by your partner even though she was pregnant is thought to detract from, rather than to enhance, your credibility.
- Even if you genuinely believe you have been told by an angel to leave Bethlehem there is still no independent evidence that your claim is well-founded. You say that after you had left King Herod ordered the slaughter of all the boys in Bethlehem and its vicinity under the age of 2 years. However, although we are aware of several criticisms of King Herod's human rights record there is no evidence from any source to support your claim that this alleged atrocity occurred. It is thought that if this had happened there would be independent evidence in the usual human rights reports to support it.

- It is also noted that although three censuses are believed to have been organised by Caesar Augustus, none of them occurred at the time you say you were required to go to Bethlehem. Your claim that it was the first census conducted while Quirinius was Governor of Syria further undermines your case because records show that Quirinius was not Governor until some eleven years after your partner's son was born. Further there are two different accounts of the birth of your child. In one version it is said that you were visited by shepherds who claim to have heard celestial voices prompting them to visit but in the other version it is said that "wise men" from the East came to see the child. Even if the oxymoron is set aside, these stories are clearly inconsistent and undermine the credibility of your claim as a whole.

- In the light of these discrepancies, inconsistencies and your inability to provide independent evidence to add substance to your claim, it is not accepted that your child is at the slightest risk from the authorities in Judah.

- However, even if there is some credibility in your claim, you can reasonably be expected to establish yourself in Israel where King Herod has no authority, rather than in Judea where King Herod is tetrarch. Indeed, some sources known to the Secretary of State suggest that Nazareth is in Israel rather than Judea and you have no reason to remain in part of Palestine where King Herod has authority. This is particularly so as you are understood to be a carpenter and joiner and therefore have a transferable employment skill which should help you establish yourself and maintain your family.

- Further the Roman authorities have authority throughout and the region and are proud of their sophisticated system of law. You should be able to avail yourself of its protection.

- It is not accepted that the parents of children hated by the King are a social group within the meaning of the

Convention and so you do not qualify for protection under the Convention, even if there is any truth in your claim.

- In the circumstances you do not qualify for asylum or humanitarian protection. You have identified no policy qualifying you for any kind of discretionary leave. Removal would not infringe any of your protected human rights.

- Regard has been had to the best interests of your partner's child. Although there is some concern about his being brought up by a "father" who has made such extravagant claims, there is no evidence that you are mentally incapable of caring for the child and we conclude that his best interests lie in his remaining with his carers.

- We have carefully considered your claim but remain of the opinion that your removal from the country is appropriate.

Yours sincerely,

***

NOTE

1   This is a *'send up'* written by a Senior Immigration Judge Jonathan Perkins to remind us of what could have happened, if the application for asylum by Jesus' father, Joseph and the appeal from a refusal by the Home Office, had taken place in the UK in the 20th century

SOME MEMORABLE DATES AND EVENTS

1272 – 1307 Edward 1 (Plantagenet)
1307 – 1327 Edward II (Plantagenet)
1315 The great famine
1327 – 1377 Edward III (Plantagenet)
1338 (1333?) 100 Years War began
1346 Battle of Crécy
1346-8 The Great Plague
1355 Battle of Poitiers
1377 – 99 Richard II (Plantagenet)
1381 The (so named) Peasant's Revolt
1399 – 1413 Henry IV (House of Lancaster)
1458 - end of 100 years' War (116 years!)
1509 – 1547 Henry VIII (Tudor)
1540 Act to limit sanctuary
1537 – 1553 Edward VI
1548 Dissolution the 'Chantries
1604 - 1625 James I (Stuart)
1623 abolition of Sanctuary

GLOSSARY

Afard	=	afraid
Afor	=	before
Badgeman	=	licensed beggar
Blast	=	small beer
Book	=	Bible
Bullock Walloper	=	drover
Butter badger	=	early postman cum newsman
Cucking-stool	=	*Stool of Repentance*, for punishment of disorderly women, <u>scolds</u>, and dishonest tradesmen
"Daneshead"	=	the football, named after the hated Danes
Ewage	=	toll for passage by water
Exbed	=	axle bed on a wagon or cart
Flesher	=	butcher
Gammel	=	to play or lark
Gong	=	cesspit
Kersey	=	broadcloth
Kessimas	=	Christmas
Jake	=	cesspit
Lappide	=	wrapped
Leuga	=	roughly 1 ½ mile, outer sanctuary limit

Mel doll	=	corn stalks in form of a sheaf dressed in harvester clothes and with flowers
Melsa	=	Meaux (Priory)
Passage	=	fee for traveller with wares for sale
Pesage	=	weighing fee
Pavage	=	toll for street paving
Pontage	=	bridge toll
renky	=	having something like a fit
Rewe	=	repent
Souter	=	cobbler
Stallage	=	stall licence fee
Strake	=	strike or hit
Strakes	=	iron plates fixed to the rim of a cartwheel
Tenting	=	minding cattle or horses
Wicken wood	=	supposed power against witches

BIBLIOGRAPHY

UK – General.

Archives Ordinance 1555 Minstrels Gild

Armstrong Kate *Roots of Faith; The Great Transformation*. Knopf 2011

Baker J. Ecclesiastical Law Journal Vol 2 issue 6 1990 *The English Law of Sanctuary* pp 8-13: and Sutton T. *Modern Sanctuary* ELJo Vol I 1996 pp 487-92.

Chambers EK. *The Medieval Stage* Vol II 1903 OUP

Cole T ed. *Queens Remembrancer in Exchequer Documents Illustrative of English History* in 13 & 14th centuries 1 V fcp fo 1814.

Collingwood RG *The Idea of History* 1946 OUP.

Calender Patent Rolls vv 10-1354/58 HMSO 1916 202 V 13 1364/67 Close Rolls 1337-39 HMSO 1900 v 4 p267,372.

Craig H. *English Religious Drama of the Middle Ages* Clarendon Press 1955.

Davidson C. (Ed)*The York Corpus Christi Plays*. De Haas E Vol 87 p 147

Dyer C. *Making a Living in the Middle Ages* Yale University Press 2002.

Galbraith V H, Hunter V eds. *Anonimalle Chronicle 1333-1381.*

Gross C. ed. *Select cases from Coroners Rolls* Selden London.1896

Hardison O B. *Christian Rite & Christian Drama in the Middle Ages* 1965 John Hopkins press.

McGrath A *John Habgood Religion and Science. An Undivided Mind. 2021*

Herodotus Book VI ch 80.

Hershey Andrew H ed. *Special Eyre Rolls of Hugh Bigod* V.131 Selden Society (2021).

Hilton RH ed. *Bond Men made Free: Medieval Peasant Movements the English Rising of 1381* Routledge 2003.

HMSO 1916 pp 59,98 1381-5 pp 35,C1377-81 pp 523-4,C 1381-5 p 136.

Jordan WC, "A Fresh Look at Medieval Sanctuary," in Ruth Mazo Karras, et al., eds., Law and the Illicit in Medieval Europe (Philadelphia) University of Pennsylvania Press, 2008), 17-32

Jusserand JJ. *English Wayfaring Life in the Middle Ages* Classic Report

Knight S and Ohlgren T eds *Robin Hood and other Outlaw Tales* 1997 Kalamazoo

Kings Bench Book 9/1069 BB 2 fo210, 27/484 m25. KB 27/487(Poll Tax)

Lambert J M. *Two Thousand Years of Gild Life* 1891 Brown & Sons

McSheffrey S *Crime, Mercy and Politics in English Courts, 1400-1550* 2017 OUP 1200-1259 *Historia Anglorum* Paris M Vii Ed p109 Ed Madden D F 1866.

Matthew P. ed. *Historia Anglorum* vol 2 1189 Longmans.

Mazzinghi TJ de. *Sanctuaries* (Classic Reprint) 2018 Lulu Press

Mount T. *A Year in the Life of Medieval England* 2019 Amberley Publishing.

Musson A. *Boundaries of the Law, Geography, Gender & Jurisdiction in Medieval and Modern Europe 2005* Routledge

Orme N. *English Schools in the Middle Ages* Methuen 1973

Olson T. *Sanctuary & Penitential Rebirth in Central Middle Ages.* 2005 Routledge.

Palliser DM. *The Cambridge Urban History of Britain 600-1540 V I.*

Pegge S. *Sketch of the History of Asylum* Letter 1785. 8 British Periodicals 1787.

Reynolds S. *An Introduction to the History of English Medieval Towns* 1977 OUP

Riley HT ed. *Chronica Annales de Johannes de Trokelowe et Henrici de Blandeforde* 2013 CUP

Rolls of Itinerant Justices. NA Just/1/ 56m.44d, 95A, 174.m 27d229,274m

Sanctuary Register Harl. Mss British Museum 4292 xvi pp xxxv-lv and V II

Shoemaker K. *Sanctuary & Crime in the Middle Ages*, 2011 Fordham.

Skeat Ed. *Pierce the Ploughman's Crede* 1876.[Wolfe's edition of *Pierce the Ploughman's Crede*, printed in 1553]

Stones E L G. *The Folvilles of Ashley Folville Leicester and their Associates in Crime*. RHS 5th Ser 7 (1957).

Strutt J. *The Sports & Pastimes of the people of England* 1801 Methuen.

Stubbs W. *Constitutional History of England* V ii p 217.1875[CUP 2012]

Sturt G. *The Wheelwright's Shop* 1923 abridged Selections in The Craftsmen's Series ed Collins A F CUP 19.

Trenholme N M. *The Right of Sanctuary in England* Missouri Press 1903

Tuchmann B. *A Distant Mirror* BW Knopf 1978.

Westra L, Juss SS, Scovazzi P *Towards a Refugee Oriented Right of Asylum* 2011 Ashgate

Year Books 30 Edw 1.7 Hen I. Notebook 32 Hussey CJ. Carlyll Rep ii708.

Beverley

Allison KJ. ed. Royal Historical Society New Series, Vol. 19 (1905),. 79-99 Victoria Country History Yorks and East Riding vol 6 Beverley

Bond A. *ed Chronica Monasterii* Vv. I, II, III 1866-68, *et Melsa*

Brown P. *Old Beverley* EYorks Local History Soc 1983.

Browne H B *The Story of the East Riding of Yorkshire* A Brown & Sons 1912.

Burgess Oath. Burgess Rolls 1835,1905,1909 f

Cook D. *Beverley's Timber-Framed Buildings* Blackthorn Press 2022.

Flower C T. *The Beverley Town Riots, 1381-2* RHS Vol. 19 1905 pp.7999 https://doi.org/10.2307/3678228

Hall E & I. *Historic Beverley* Wm Sessions 1974.

Hopkins P. *History of Beverley* Blackthorn 2011.

Kirby M. *Beverley- a Town of Refuge* Parish Council Committee 2020.

Kermode JI. *Merchants Overseas Trade etc in York, Beverley, Hull 1380-1500* 2-13 https://doi.org/10.1179/007817287790176082

Leach B. *A Clerical Strike at Beverley Minster in 14th Century* Beverley Minster (E. Surtees Society. (1898-1903).

Leach A F. *Memorials of Beverley Minster: the Chapter Act Book of the Collegiate Church of S. John of Beverley, A.D. 1286-1347*

Leach A F. ed. *Beverley Town Documents 1900*

Lee P & Hick P. *Beverley Town Trail Revisited* 2011 Hart & Clough.

McCutcheon K L *Transactions of the Yorkshire Fairs and Markets to the end of the 18th Century* Thesis 1935.

Miller K & others. *Beverley: An archaeological and architectural study* Royal Commission Supp. Ser 4 HMSO 1982.

Neave S and Ellis S. *Historical Atlas of East Yorkshire* 1996. University of Hull

Poulson G. *Beverlac: the Antiquities & History of the Town of Beverley etc* Vol.1 Scaum (Longman) 1829.

Purvis J S. *From Minster to Market Place* St Anthony Press 1969.

Wormald P. *Beverley Town Trail Medieval Crafts and Guilds* 2010 https://www.visiteastyorkshire.co.uk/things-to-do/medieval-guilds

USA & Canada

Bau I. *This Ground is Holy: Church Sanctuary and Central American* NY 1985 Paulist Press.

Golden R. & McConnell. M *Sanctuary: the New Underground Railroad* Maryknoll, N.Y.: Orbis Books

Hudson G & others *A History of the Memories of the 'Sanctuary City In Toronto Canada*, WP no 2020/5 Ryerson Centre for Immigration and Settlement. A Pilot Study on Sanctuary City Policy in Toronto Canada Working Paper 2017/1 RCIS.

Lippert R Sanctuary, Sovereignty, Sacrifice: Canadian Sanctuary Incidents, Power, and Law 2006, UBC Press

Marfleet P. *Understanding 'Sanctuary': Faith and Traditions of Asylum* Journal of Refugee Studies, Vol 24/3 2011, Pages 440–455, https://doi.org/10.1093/jrs/fer040

Robinson V ed. *Refugee Crisis: British and Canadian Responses* (London): Macmillan, 1993).

Marina V. *Sanctuary: Reviving an Old Concept* Los Angeles Times 17.11.85.

Moffette D & Ridgley J *Migration & Society* Vol 1/1 Berghahn Books Inc 2018

Stastny C & Tyrnauer G *Sanctuary in Canada* in Robinson V ed

Robinson V *The International Refugee Crisis: British and Canadian Responses* Palgrave Macmillan 1993

New York Times 8.6.86 https://www.imdb.com/title/tt0965394

https://www.youtube.com/watch?v=PkpKQRIjyaw

INDEX

147

~~~~~~~